Foreign Aid's Effects on Development and Human Security in Kenya

Foreign Aid's Effects on Development and Human Security in Kenya

John Bosco Ngendakurio

LEXINGTON BOOKS
Lanham • Boulder • New York • London

Published by Lexington Books
An imprint of The Rowman & Littlefield Publishing Group, Inc.
4501 Forbes Boulevard, Suite 200, Lanham, Maryland 20706
www.rowman.com

86-90 Paul Street, London EC2A 4NE

British Library Cataloguing in Publication Information Available

Library of Congress Cataloging-in-Publication Data Available

ISBN 978-1-66694-370-2 (cloth: alk. paper) | ISBN 978-1-66694-371-9 (ebook)

∞™ The paper used in this publication meets the minimum requirements of American National Standard for Information Sciences—Permanence of Paper for Printed Library Materials, ANSI/NISO Z39.48-1992.

Contents

Preface vii

Introduction: Kenya, a Major Recipient of Foreign Aid 1

1 The Concept of Human Security and the Politics of International Law 7

2 Key Human Security and Development Problems in Kenya 19

3 The Legacies of British Colonial Rule and Neo-Colonial Practices in Kenya 45

4 History and Processes of Foreign Aid 67

5 Bypass Theory: An Effective Way to Prevent Foreign Aid's Capture in Bad Governance and Corruptive Practices 81

Conclusion: Discussions and Recommendations 91

Bibliography 101

Index 123

About the Author 125

Preface

The central question this book addresses is: *How does foreign aid affect human security in Kenya?* More than USD1 trillion has been transferred to Africa from rich countries in development-related aid in the last 50 years, but evidence indicates that poverty levels continue to surge upward. Kenya, as a Sub-Saharan African country and recipient of large-scale foreign aid, is a microcosm of what is happening in Africa and a good place to start a thorough investigation into the effectiveness of foreign aid to poor countries. Apart from providing a geopolitical analysis of the long-term effects of colonialism in a key African country, this book on the foreign-aid schemes intends to contribute further knowledge and firsthand information necessary to reshape and improve related processes and practices, for the benefit of both the donors and the intended beneficiaries. The content in this book derives from my PhD thesis, where a qualitative research methodology involving traveling to Kenya to conduct face-to-face, semi-structured interviews with local Kenyans and residents who have direct knowledge about the foreign-aid scheme's processes and practices was the most appropriate method to investigate individuals' lived experiences. The locals' original accounts have been triangulated with the material from primary and secondary sources to inform this book. I take this opportunity to unreservedly express my gratitude to each person who has contributed to this book project, especially the lovely people of Kenya, for their warm welcome, generosity, time, support, trust, and openness as they shared their insights about the foreign-aid scheme and key human security issues in Kenya with me. I am deeply grateful to my PhD supervisors—Associate Professor Georgina Murray and Professor Emeritus David Peetz. I was overwhelmed by their support, patience, and understanding. Thank you! This book is dedicated to you and my entire family.

Introduction

Kenya, a Major Recipient of Foreign Aid

Using Kenya as a case study, this book was designed to close the information gap in the literature and outline recommendations for what needs to be done to improve the effectiveness of foreign aid. It has answered the central question of *How does foreign aid affect human security in Kenya?*, and three subquestions; that is, *What is the state of human security in Kenya? What factors, including foreign aid, have influenced human security in Kenya? What factors explain the influence of foreign aid on income security in Kenya?*

Kenya is a major recipient of foreign aid, and the amount of money received from foreign governments and other international donors continues to upsurge (McCormick & Schmitz 2011, p. 156). Between 2000 and 2005 alone, Kenya experienced at least an 83 percent increase in donors who wished to support the industrialization sector and a 325 percent increase in donors whose funding was directed to projects designed to promote political reforms. Consequently, inclusive industrialization projects rose from 8 to 33, whereas good governance projects rose from 5 to 79 (McCormick & Schmitz 2011, p. 156). Despite this increase in funding, the effectiveness of foreign aid in reducing poverty in poor countries, especially in Sub-Saharan Africa, has largely been disputed (Moyo 2017). This book looks at evidence suggesting that the scheme has complemented the Kenyan government's work, improving its public perceptions and legitimacy (Dolan 2020, p. 145).

Donors have had to look at new, more effective forms of delivery. The British, for example, have tried a bilateral aid scheme that has recently changed its focus, bringing development and trade closer together (Islam 2019). This book looks at these changing policies and critically analyzes the suggestion that, rather than enhancing poor countries' foreign-aid dependency, the recently established British foreign-aid agenda prioritizes the empowerment of the aid-receiving countries, helping them to reach sustainable development and trade their way out of poverty (Islam 2019). It is claimed that, by providing the policymakers with the skills necessary to develop the same attributes that helped the United Kingdom to attract investments, the British foreign-aid agenda ensures trade deals are sealed on a stable basis. Kenya is one of the target countries (Islam 2019).

On the other hand, Chinese engagement in Kenya has progressively increased, with China supporting short- and long-term educational programs such as enterprise-based training through university-to-university cooperation (King 2010, p. 489). Such cooperation dates from the dawn of Kenyan independence in the 1960s, and the number of student beneficiaries has substantially increased in the recent past (King 2010, p. 489). Similarly, the Kenyan government's strategy, Vision 2030, which emphasizes infrastructure investment, is mainly funded by China. Consequently, Chinese firms have rapidly emerged, becoming some of the most significant employers in the country (Plummer 2019, p. 680). This book investigates if such substantial engagement in Africa is determined by Chinese historic allegiance to Third World solidarity, making it the greatest supporter of African and Asian governments with a socialist orientation (cf. Harris 2018, p. 1716), or if it is designed primarily to safeguard Chinese interests in the continent.

It is also claimed that non-governmental organizations (NGOs) have been instrumental in mitigating gaps in servicesservice delivery in Africa in collaboration with the host governments. For example, they have developed new energy solutions at local levels, a move that has seen improvement in small-scale and localized production of electricity (MacLean & Brass 2015, p. 58). In a typical Kenyan context, NGOs practicing community-driven techniques have successfully organized energy cooperatives that can manage a village-scale hydroelectricity station with the capacity to power several local communities (MacLean & Brass 2015, p. 58). In the vital sector of public health, NGOs in Kenya have demonstrated the will and the capabilities to increase their reach, offering the much-needed technical support and boosting the overall healthcare system's performance (Suchman, Hart & Montagu 2018, pp. 778–779).

The complementary work carried out by NGOs can be evidenced through their success in reducing the spread of HIV/AIDS in Kenya. The Western funding to the HIV/AIDS sector has resulted in special arrangements for sex workers in the form of clinics and drop-in centers in major towns. These centers provide free screenings, treatment, and medication (Česnulytė 2015, p. 1162). Access to healthcare facilities is particularly important in poor and developing countries. It remains one of the core factors shaping the potency of some of the most important Millennium Development Goals (MDGs). Better access and utilization of health services in Kenya means equity of healthcare in a country significantly affected by the disease burden (Feikin et al. 2009,

p. 54). Several NGOs have also established vocational training, education, and business development skills, targeting the most vulnerable members of the community, including but not limited to sex workers (Česnulytė 2015, p. 1162). This book objectively evaluates the role of these NGOs in alleviating Kenyan human security and development issues, especially poverty.

The inability or unwillingness of the Kenyan government to fully cater to the needs of its marginalized citizens has left local religious leaders with no choice but to step in and provide short- and long-term services (Agensky 2020, p. 589). This phenomenon is common in other Sub-Saharan African countries, but Kenya remains the headquarters of most faith-based organizations (Agensky 2020, p. 589). The Kenyan Khadi Courts, for example, apply Islamic Law of personal status, and they were entrenched in the Kenyan constitution in the aftermath of the country's independence in 1963 (Cussac 2008, p. 289). Similarly, rural education programs are being delivered by the National Christian Council of Kenya (NCCK). Several other NGOs operate in the region, and they have evolved from church-based relief and development structures. Their work is mainly funded by Western donors as a part of the foreign-aid scheme (Agensky 2020, p. 589).

It is further claimed that international non-governmental organizations (INGOs) such as Oxfam have been operating in Kenya since the 1960s, providing long-term development aid and emergency relief. They have also engaged in peacebuilding and social cohesion projects, actively campaigning for better governance and equity (Oxfam 2017). Oxfam works collaboratively with the Government of Kenya, civil society, communities, and international and private actors in their attempt to alleviate poverty (Oxfam 2017). Additionally, aid officials and other international actors have historically applied pressure on the Kenyan government to do more in the areas of peace, democracy, and justice, even if the international community often overestimates the ability of Western actors to influence policies in African countries (Brown & Raddatz 2014, p. 44).

Local and international NGOs have quickly proliferated in Kenya over the past two decades, with thousands of NGOs operating in the main sectors affecting Kenyans' daily life (Hershey 2013, p. 671). But what has this rapid NGOs' proliferation meant for the Kenyan indigenous populations? Has such growth stemmed from pressures of the neo-liberal approach coupled with the increasing prioritization of NGOs by Western donors? Whatever the reason might be, it remains unclear how the effects of this approach interact with local politics to create a domestic space in which these organizations could thrive and maximize outcomes for the beneficiaries (Hershey 2013, p. 671). That's why, as a part of my qualitative data collection through semi-structured interviews, I heavily investigated individuals' lived experiences as they were presented through feelings, ideas, perceptions, attitudes, and thoughts. This was the most appropriate method to find answers to the study's main research question of *How does foreign aid affect human security in Kenya?* Qualitative research methodology involves a thorough examination of phenomena that impact the lived reality of the research participants in a particular social context. The method has progressively evolved over the recent decades to attain a high level of credibility due to its proven track record in exploring the human condition and its numerous truths (Mills & Birks 2014).

The choice of the qualitative research methodology for this study was sparked by the need to explore local and indigenous perspectives in relation to the effectiveness of foreign aid in Kenya. The qualitative research methodology design empowers participants by providing them with a unique opportunity to share their views on a topic that matters to them and their families (Dodgson 2017, p. 355). Participants are further requested to reflect on the "how" and "why" questions in relation to specific phenomena that occur in complex contexts where variables are not easily controlled. Qualitative research proves to be particularly important when examining processes that involve multiple stakeholders with different perspectives, socio-economic, cultural, historical, and political contexts, as well as conflicting interests (Trainor & Graue 2014, p. 268).

Semi-structured interviews with participants make it easier for researchers to understand cultural nuances and political sensitivities that might create ethical and methodological challenges (Kabranian-Melkonian 2015, p. 717), while also enabling them to explore complex issues involving human behaviors, actions, and related consequences. Most importantly, it makes it possible to fully answer questions by giving detailed explanations of what happened and the key underlying factors of a given situation (Kelly 2017, p. 933). Therefore, an increasing number of research fields have integrated qualitative research approaches as they can deal with questions and topics that quantitative and other methodologies cannot accommodate in a holistic, interpretive, and relational manner (Burdine, Thorne & Sandhu 2021, p. 336).

Qualitative research methodology was further appropriate to mitigate local challenges and procedural gaps. Some Kenyan populations and low-level authorities are hard to reach (Benoit et al. 2005, p. 265). The qualitative research methodology helped the researcher to establish direct contact with the initial participants, progressively developing a greater understanding of local expectations and fostering relationships with community-based stakeholders, including major organizations operating in and around Kenya. This tactic has proven to make the research process smoother (Benoit et al. 2005, p. 265), and it helped the researcher understand the research site and setting.

The participants in this research were average Kenyan residents and citizens in different social classes and backgrounds, Kenyan authorities, civil society activists, local staff working in local and international NGOs, expatriates, diplomats, senior security and military officers, high school and university students, religious leaders, and academics mainly in the fields of global economics, political science, international relations, and security studies. The indigenous sample consisted of both adult men and women from different districts, tribes, religious, social, economic, and political backgrounds, all of whom had direct knowledge about the foreign-aid scheme as administrators, frontline workers, or beneficiaries. The researcher conducted 61 interviews, 4 of which were not audio-recorded. Four interviews occurred in Brisbane, and all these participants are professionals who have administered foreign aid as beneficiaries or donors. All the direct quotes used in this book derive from the views and insights from these participants. All interviews used in this book have been anonymized to safeguard the privacy of participants.

Bypass theory was used and tested to evaluate how the work of local and international organizations operating in Kenya has affected the average Kenyans' health and well-being. Bypass theory suggests that, while government-to-government aid remains significant in Sub-Saharan Africa, bypassing governments is more impactful at the grassroots level (Dietrich 2016, p. 67). This book critically evaluated the effectiveness of this theory, which implies giving aid funding to non-state actors operating in the field to reduce the risk of aid capture in bad governance and corruption (Dietrich 2016, p. 67). It is largely anticipated that the high level of international engagement will have a positive impact on Kenyans' overall human security and development, at least to a certain extent (cf. Sachs 2014).

Chapter 1

The Concept of Human Security and the Politics of International Law

The concept of human security shifts away from the traditional way of thinking about security (Camilleri 2012, p. 12). It extends beyond national defense to include other threats that directly impact the welfare of ordinary people (Inglehart & Norris 2012, p. 71). It emphasizes the fundamental freedoms that are vital for a decent human life, demonstrating the need to protect people from threats and undesirable situations. Therefore, processes that empower individuals with strengths and aspirations are central. Human security is about the creation of favorable environments for members of the community to thrive economically, socially, environmentally, militarily, culturally, and politically. Such conditions equip individuals with the building blocks necessary to improve their livelihoods, promoting human dignity (Camilleri 2012, p. 13).

Human dignity is undermined when members of the community fail to achieve economic security; that is, when they are living in perpetual poverty as a result of unemployment and low or insecure income. It is also threatened when the food available to people is insufficient in quantity and quality, leading to health-related vulnerabilities such as infectious diseases and malnutrition (Tadjbakhsh & Chenoy [1965] 2006, p. 128). The degradation of the ecosystems—water, land, air—and natural disasters also cause a significant threat to human security. Therefore, accomplished human security implies that individuals can enjoy freedom from fear, wants, and physical violence, providing them with the opportunity to live in a society and systems that honor their basic human rights (Tadjbakhsh & Chenoy [1965] 2006, p. 128). Such freedom is difficult to achieve in Africa, a continent known for its numerous and complex human security and development problems (Hübschle 2011, p. 81).

HUMAN SECURITY AND DEVELOPMENT PROBLEMS IN THE AFRICAN CONTEXT

Africans suffer from a range of complex human security and development problems, many of which are of transnational nature. African governments' perceived weaknesses in terms of law enforcement, poor border control, and inadequate strategies to tackle terrorism provide an environment for terrorist networks to flourish (Hübschle 2011, p. 81). Besides, global terrorist networks such as Al-Qaeda and Islamic States (IS) have renewed their interest in Africa, where they compete for influence at the expense of the average citizens. They have elaborated tactics, making it easier to cross borders in what experts have labeled "terrorism without borders" (Morumbasi & Amuhaya 2016, p. 265). This is particularly alarming in the contemporary world, where conflicts are so interconnected that they become transnational due to the forces of globalization. Consequently, a local problem effectively becomes global, impacting the political, social, and economic order (Hrubec & Uhde 2018, p. 777).

The African continent is known for its abundant natural resources, making it vulnerable first to colonialism (Anyangwe 2017) and subsequently, neo-colonialism. Even if, in theory, all East African countries have secured independence, their economic, social, and political policies are usually dictated by foreign powers (Maekawa 2015, p. 317). Paradoxically, most of the poorest and the most troubled nations in Africa have the largest natural resources reserves. Why is this? Anyanwu (2014, p. 209) suggests that it is because the African natural resources have been the main sources of conflicts and, therefore, the continent has been hit the hardest by civil wars, registering nearly a third of the world's conflicts between 1989 and 2009. The civil war in the Democratic Republic of Congo (DRC), for example, shares several commonalities with other recent conflicts in Africa. It has led to gross violations of human rights, deaths, and family splits. It has also created a history of torture and trauma among Congolese refugees as they have been forced to take dangerous journeys, ending up in refugee camps and adversely contributing to the refugee burden in Africa and beyond (Ngendakurio 2017, p. 2). Following the recent waves of violent conflicts in the DRC between 2017 and 2019, for example, there were over 918,000 refugees of DRC origin in African countries as of February 2020 (UNHCR 2020).

The scarcity of shared resources is one of the major problems facing people in Sub-Saharan Africa. While it is widely acknowledged that water, sanitation, and hygiene are some of the most essential needs for a healthy and dignified life, Sub-Saharan Africans do not have enough access to these assets. In fact, an estimated 32 percent of its population is missing out. Approximately 102 million still use surface water while around 695 million people do not have adequate sanitation facilities, leading to several health issues, including but not limited to diarrhea (Roche, Bain & Cumming 2017, p. 3). Informal settlements in Sub-Saharan Africa are affected the most due to unsustainable water systems, poor shelter, and limited sanitation services. Initiatives to improve these trends have largely failed because of cultural practices, numerous actors with conflicting interests, and hostile societal or governance structures (Silvestri et al. 2018).

The recent epidemics and the emergence of infectious diseases such as Ebola, cholera, yellow fever, Zika, dengue, and Rift Valley fever have put to test the capacity of African nations to respond to the increasing health burdens, revealing key weaknesses in the healthcare systems (Olu et al. 2017). While Sub-Saharan Africa is already strained in its capacity to cater to the health needs of its citizens, the burden of chronic, non-communicable diseases on the continent has increased (Wang et al. 2015). In 2019, evidence suggested that non-communicable diseases' prevalence was rising fastest in lower-income settings. Poor countries also endured more devastating outcomes compared to greater powers, with cardiovascular diseases, cancers, chronic respiratory diseases, diabetes, and mental illnesses continuing to upsurge (Juma et al. 2019). Additionally, healthcare costs in Africa have continued to rise in a population with the lowest purchasing power (Wang et al. 2015).

Sub-Saharan Africa is home to almost one-third of the world's poor (Verster 2015). Its monthly per capital Gross Domestic Product (GDP) is estimated at 10 to 20 times less than what pertains in the Global North, and its contribution to the World GDP has been stagnant at 2 percent since 2005 (Obeng-Odoom 2020, p.137). Poverty in Sub-Saharan Africa is a wicked problem. Even though a range of projects has been initiated to change the poverty rates, most positive developments fail to materialize because of the high levels of debt, unemployment, and poor infrastructure (Verster 2015). Consequently, Africans continue to suffer because of poverty that undermines individuals' well-being. The lack of income often compromises health, nutrition, education, and housing outcomes. Poverty leads to inequality of opportunity, leading to powerlessness and vulnerability and widening the inequality gap. The high level of poverty in Africa has forced a great number of Africans to migrate to other countries seeking greener pastures. But even these migrations have dire consequences as they further increase inequalities, particularly in rural areas (Dwumfour, Agbloyor & Abor 2017, p. 2033).

Even more devastating, the historic imperialist practices were designed to maintain Africa in perpetual poverty (Broughton 2018, p. 19). The exploitation of African resources began with slavery centuries ago and it was further enhanced after the Berlin Conference, with the European superpowers dividing Africa among themselves (Idejiora-Kalu 2019, p. 99). This move enabled the richest and the most powerful players in the world order to exploit and drain African resources unhindered for a long time. These practices did not stop with African nations securing independence. Only the form and the nature of exploitation have changed (Broughton 2018, p. 19). Even if Africa were to revolt today, they do not have what it takes to meaningfully compete in the global market. Technology has always been a key factor in class organization and formulation, making it possible for the Industrial Revolution to create new ways to organize labor and amass wealth. Unfortunately for Africa, those who own and control the new technologies use them to organize labor in a way that benefits the most powerful in the chain (Harris 2015, p. 4).

A transnational capitalist class (TCC) has emerged as a part of the world's bourgeoisie that represents the transnational capital. The TCC's agenda is mainly the construction and enhancement of a new global capitalist bloc, which consists of economic and political forces that have become dominant in the sector of the ruling class throughout the world (Robinson & Harris 2000, p. 11), and logically, this bloc was designed to protect the interests of the most powerful in the world order. Besides, the solutions to the most pressing threats, including poverty, require collaborations and coordination between developed and developing nations. Unfortunately, these relationships are largely shaped by enduring inequalities that often impede the most appropriate actions (Reese, Berthold & Steffens 2012, p. 683). Consequently, the poor continue to suffer because of income inequality and poverty, which lead to a chain of other human security threats such as crime (Hooghe et al. 2010, p. 1).

The abundance and rapid proliferation of small arms within the African continent, Falode (2020, p. 158) argues, contribute to economic, social, and political insecurity. They also facilitate major transnational crimes such as drugs and human trafficking. Cattle rustling, for example, had traditionally been driven by a small group of criminals invading pastoralist communities with arrows and spears to expropriate the cattle for meat or small-scale sales. To date, the practice has become an organized criminal activity, with rustlers forming vast and sophisticated networks that cut across various nationalities (Ibrahim et al. 2016, p. 2). On the other hand, there are several cyber-enabled crimes that emanate from Africa, especially Nigeria, including financial fraud and hacking (Whitty 2018, p. 97).

Unique to Africa are the level, nature, and intensity of crimes committed. For example, Taylor, Bradbury-Jones and Lund (2019, p. 13) argue that witchcraft-related murders of children born with albinism are on the rise in the continent. Similarly, African children who are visually impaired are not only socially isolated, but they are also potential victims of witchcraft-related violence. Some members of the community allegedly use their body parts in lucky charms believed to bring good fortune (Taylor, Bradbury-Jones & Lund

2019, p. 13). Extrajudicial killings are also common in Africa. For example, assassinations by the police have taken the lives of thousands of young men over the past decade in Kenya, where, in locations like the Mathare Slum, the police simply shoot crime suspects instead of taking them to court (van Stapele 2016, p. 302). Further south in South Africa, mob justice has increasingly become a major concern. It occurs when angry mobs attack and kill the suspects, sometimes in front of an outnumbered and powerless police force (Baloyi 2015, p. 1).

Some typically African cultural practices and beliefs endanger the most vulnerable members of the community, especially women and children. Children fall victim to human sacrifice rituals intended for healing, dealing with misfortunes, or preventing unfortunate events. The practices imply removing the child's body parts, blood, or tissues while they are still alive. The removed body parts are either buried or eaten in the belief that the fortune and well-being of others in the community will improve (Mpyakulukngu & Bui 2018, p. 12). Children also fall victim to the mistaken belief that sexual intercourse with a virgin cures a HIV-infected person. Such beliefs have put young children at higher risk for rape (Meel 2003, p. 85). Similarly, female genital mutilation is still a major contributor to high morbidity and mortality among African females. There have been several efforts to curb the practice, but they have largely failed because it is deeply embedded into religious and community beliefs passed on from generation to generation (Obiora, Maree & Nkosi-Mafutha 2020).

Widows in Sub-Saharan Africa are subject to a range of plights. They face daily discrimination, stigmatization, oppression, and deprivation at the hands of their in-laws (Ude & Njoku 2017, p. 1512). Additionally, widow inheritance, that is, being forced to marry the late husband's relative, is one of the major underlying factors of the higher prevalence of HIV/AIDS among women in Sub-Saharan Africa (Ude & Njoku 2017, p. 1515). The rights of widows in terms of land and other assets' inheritance are limited in Africa. While significant activism has been initiated in the attempt to secure legal rights of women, such high-level legal battles by women are hard-fought mainly because any suggestions of equal rights to inherit land historically face overwhelming resistance in Sub-Saharan Africa, enhancing gender inequality (Dancer 2017, p. 292).

Gender inequality, Bataka (2020, p. 517) argues, generates an imbalance in the distribution of power. It leads to inequality of opportunity in education, adversely impacting women's social capital, participation, political, social, and financial autonomy (Bataka 2020, p. 517). It has also become the main barrier to achieving freedom from fear and violence both in personal and professional life. Women are generally discriminated against in the labor market—they are usually paid less simply because they are women (Bataka

2020, p. 517). The high level of poverty within female populations in Sub-Saharan Africa is attributed to the continent's high levels of gender inequality (Workneh 2020, p. 150) due to the existing inegalitarian laws, norms, and traditions toward women. Such conditions continue to impede human and economic development and that is one of the reasons why Sub-Saharan Africa lags economically, with its female population particularly vulnerable (Elu 2013, p. 105).

Child marriage, a phenomenon common in poor and developing countries, is largely linked to poor educational, socio-economic, and health outcomes for women and female children. Despite improvements in female education in Sub-Saharan Africa, early marriages remain a reality (Corno, Hildebrandt & Voena 2020, p. 880). Child marriage is a human rights violation that continues to impede the victim's livelihood with lifelong implications. It not only prevents the female child from choosing her own life partner, maturing, and bonding with peers, but it can also lead to an increased risk of sexually transmitted diseases, premature birth, or deaths (Nour 2006, p. 1644).

Driven by greed or despair, some Sub-Saharan African parents choose when their children marry. Income shocks usually affect the age of marriage as dowry becomes an important source of income that helps to provide for the woman's family (Corno, Hildebrandt & Voena 2020, p. 879). Furthermore, arranged marriages where parents choose marital partners on behalf of their adult children are also common in Africa, preventing adult individuals from making some of the most important decisions affecting their lives (Munshi 2017, p. 36). Without a meaningful mindset change across all levels of society, it remains difficult to achieve substantial change in Sub-Saharan Africa mainly due to limited opportunities for quality education (Agyepong et al. 2017, p. 2804).

One of the post-2015 Sustainable Development Goals emphasizes higher education. The goal specifically aims at ensuring equal access to affordable technical, vocational, and tertiary education, including university for all by 2030. Sub-Saharan Africans are furthest from achieving this goal (Ilie & Rose 2016, p. 436). Barakabitze et al. (2019, p. 2) argue that any initiatives to improve the quality of education in Sub-Saharan Africa face numerous barriers. For example, while information and communication technology (ICT) has been introduced in most African countries, its adoption is among the slowest due to ineffective policies, the lack of relevant tools, and adequate infrastructure such as internet, electricity, software, and hardware devices. The continent also faces issues of teacher capacity and, most importantly, financial resources (Barakabitze et al. 2019, p. 2). As such, even the *Education for All* campaign from the 1990s achieved little over decades in Sub-Saharan Africa. The region registered alarmingly low levels of student achievements and high levels of school dropouts, leading to system inefficiency (Dembélé & Oviawe 2007, p. 473).

Brain drain remains an inescapable reality for African countries. The lack of opportunities for professionals, coupled with Westerners' tactics of luring the best talents away from poor countries, have enhanced the trends (Twisselmann 2005, p. 780). The best African brains mostly migrate to the United States (US), United Kingdom (UK), Canada, and Europe. Therefore, it is practically impossible for Africa to achieve any significant development (Adesote & Osunkoya 2018, p. 396). On the other hand, superpowers continue to fuel conflicts in poor countries out of greed as their arms trade agreements depend on social troubles (Twisselmann 2005, p. 780). Consequently, failure to optimize community-level sustainability impedes efforts to protect the society, particularly children (Peterman et al. 2017, p. 1049).

Physical, emotional, and sexual violence affect around 1 billion children per year. It has detrimental effects on children's development, adversely impacting on their ability to learn. Such experiences take children's rights to a healthy and productive life away. Children in poor countries are hit the hardest, as evidence suggests, four out of five children aged between two and fourteen experience some form of physical violence at least once a month (Peterman et al. 2017, p. 1050). For example, the threats faced by street children in Africa are unique in nature and character. They are at higher risk for disease burden because of their living conditions. They also have difficulties in securing food and other basic needs, particularly shelter. Basically, they live in half-destroyed or abandoned houses, under bridges, or simply in the open air (Cumber & Tsoka-Gwegweni 2015). Such living conditions are particularly detrimental in regions such as Sub-Saharan Africa, known for its extreme heatwaves because of climate change (Harrington & Otto 2020, p. 796).

Sub-Saharan Africa is more vulnerable to the effects of climate change than any other region in the world due to multiple biophysical, socio-economic, and political stressors that impede its adaptive capabilities. Therefore, climate change has progressively become a major source of food insecurity in the region (Connolly-Boutin & Smit 2015, p. 385). The 2011 drought in East Africa caused significant loss, reportedly costing the Kenyan economy alone more than USD 12 billion (Adede et al. 2019). Extreme droughts in Sub-Saharan Africa limit pastoralists' and agro-pastoralists' ability to grow food and rear livestock as they are unable to adapt to changes in water and rain patterns (Connolly-Boutin & Smit 2015, p. 385). With so many complex human security and development issues in the continent, the African leadership must refocus on good governance to save the fragility of African nations and systems from collapsing (Adesote & Osunkoya 2018, p. 396). Ironically, even with foreign-aid projects, African leadership still fails to find durable solutions to the most pressing issues such as poverty (Moyo 2017).

Poor governance has had dire consequences for African nations' prospects for development. Diversion of funds meant for poverty alleviation and other programs by government officials is common and has resulted in the failure to deliver public goods and services in key areas such as health, infrastructure, and education (Adekoya & Razak 2016, p. 30). Leaders with corrupt records typically continue to enjoy luxurious lives at the expensive of the poor. That's why, even if some of the Sub-Saharan African countries, for example, have recently been classified among the fastest-growing economies, these trends do not reflect the lives of the average citizens; that is, the majority. Millions still languish in poverty, hunger, poor sanitation, and poor healthcare (Ayodeji & Tobi 2019, p. 6). That's why, given the level of human security threats facing most countries in Africa, the international community is obligated to step in and assist through the foreign-aid scheme under international law (Glanville 2010, p. 287).

INTERNATIONAL COMMUNITY'S RESPONSIBILITY TO PROTECT AND THE POLITICS OF INTERNATIONAL LAW

The international community has the responsibility to encourage and assist sovereign states to protect their citizens from current and imminent threats. It is also expected to take collective action where states have failed to fulfill their obligations (Glanville 2010, p. 287). Therefore, the international community's responsibility to protect enhances the unity of the human family and promotes the dignity of every human being regardless of their background. As such, individual state's right to sovereignty is tied to its willingness and ability to safeguard the health and well-being of individuals within its territory (Barbour & Gorlick 2008, p. 534). In other words, failure to provide appropriate protection to its citizens through violation or neglect renders the state's right to sovereignty void and gives the international community a legal venue to step in for appropriate action (Barbour & Gorlick 2008, p. 534).

History has demonstrated that delaying international interventions can lead to catastrophic outcomes for humanity. The aftermath of the Cold War, for example, initially raised hopes, with greater peace between sovereign states. However, intra-state crises quickly mushroomed, including genocides such as the case of Rwanda, where over one million innocent people were slaughtered in less than four months in 1994 (Adelman 2002, p. 3). As threats facing the world are wide-ranging, several international and intergovernmental organizations have been formed, covering key areas such as international economics, international security, and international law (Hurd 2011, p. 2). The top-ten organizations formed with the main objective to collectively address the world's most pressing issues under the principles of international law are the United Nations (UN), the World Trade Organization (WTO), International Monetary Fund (IMF), the European Union (EU), the World Bank (WB), the International Court of Justice (ICJ), the International Criminal Court (ICC), International Labour Organization (ILO), the African Union (AU), and the Association of Southeast Asian Nations (ASEAN) (Hurd 2011, p. 2). Organizations such as the UN have different branches, all of which cover key responsibility areas. The United Nations International Children's Emergency Fund (UNICEF) was created to ensure child protection and inclusion (UNICEF 2020), while the Food and Agricultural Organization of the UN (FAO) was created to lead international efforts to eradicate hunger (FAO 2020), just to name a few.

The fact that there are no mechanisms for the international system to effectively hold sovereign governments to account poses a significant challenge to the international community. The contemporary world is shaped by anarchy; that is, there is no central, overarching, and legitimate power to monitor or shape the behaviors of sovereign states. This condition puts sovereign governments in a position of strength as they hold legitimate monopoly to use force—authorities can do whatever they desire within their territorial boundaries and get away with it (McNamara 2019, p. 41). For example, while genocide is one of the most serious crimes, and the international community has an interest in preventing or punishing perpetrators, foreign states have limited legal venues to prevent its occurrence or to hold the relevant individuals in positions of power to account (Longobardo 2015, p. 1199).

Under International Humanitarian Law, a violent conflict between the state and non-state actors cannot be declared as an armed conflict until the violence surpasses a minimum threshold (Hathaway et al. 2016, p. 4), raising the question of "how many people must die before relevant domestic and international interventions can legally and effectively occur to stop atrocities?" A typical example is the Rwandan Genocide in 1994, where evidence suggests the UN and Belgium had forces in the country, but their mission was not given a mandate to intervene and stop the killings (BBC 2019a). Instances like this have led policymakers to question if peacekeeping missions are necessary or worth the cost in places where there is no peace to keep (Jett 2016, p. 149). Besides, the lack of a clear definition of what constitutes genocide has historically been a main cause of paralysis in the international system in terms of the relevance of the response to mass murders both in Rwanda and Sudan (Charny 2016, p. 2).

There is no enforceable law to coerce states to intervene in other countries' internal affairs or the world's most pressing problems. The refugee crisis, for example, has prompted tensions between legal principles, moral duties, and national interests (Bradley 2019, pp. 45–47). The debates about the refugee burden are centered on the obligation to admit refugees and responsibility sharing. National interests usually outweigh the moral responsibility and, therefore, most states limit their obligations (Bradley 2019, pp. 45–47). For instance, South Africa is obligated to apply international refugee law under the UN and Organisation of African Unity (OAU) Refugee Conventions to address asylum seekers' protection needs. Unfortunately, officials often purposefully ignore both domestic and international laws to protect asylum seekers and refugees' rights (Maluwa & Katz 2020, p. 130). Similarly, while it is not a crime to apply for protection, asylum seekers who arrive in Australia by boat, including those who are undoubtedly legitimate refugees to whom Australia has a legal obligation to protect under international law, are historically detained indefinitely (Sales 2015).

The United Nations High Commissioner for Refugees (UNHCR) has had to step in to provide the basic and protection needs of refugees and asylum seekers. The organization was created in the aftermath of the Second World War to help millions of refugees who had fled their homes in Europe. It has since expanded in size and activities, historically protecting over 50 million refugees, and currently operating in 135 countries. As per the 2019 financial year, its budget grew to more than USD8 billion, with over 17,324 personnel worldwide (UNHCR 2020c). Several other national and international non-governmental organizations, global movements, and the civil society have historically extended the range of citizens' action beyond the state of anarchy (Turner 1998, p. 25).

The engagement and activism by the international community based on the principles of international law have improved the well-being, safety, and dignity of the world's most vulnerable people. Even if states typically place some reservations on their international human rights treaties' ratification status, evidence suggests that a large and expanding body of international human rights treaty law is being adopted by an increasing number of governments (Hill Jr. 2016, p. 1130). For example, most governments have formally committed to respecting, protecting, and fulfilling the right to social security by ratifying human rights and ILO's Convention. This, in practice, means that signatories have now committed to guaranteeing healthcare equity and relevant social welfare assistance in case of illness, disability, unemployment, or old age (Krennerich 2014, p. 105).

The Millennium Development Goals (MDGs) constitute a framework for collective efforts by national governments and main international development bodies to improve living standards in the world (Njoh & Ananga 2016, p. 90). The MDGs' campaign between 2002 and 2015, with the objective to eradicate poverty, received overwhelming support worldwide. It was adopted by 189 UN member states, and it set several goals including, but not limited to, access to safe and sustainable water and basic sanitation, including hygiene. These goals were of particular importance in low-income countries where poor quality drinking water is linked to a range of adverse economic and health outcomes (Weststrate et al. 2018, p. 796). MDGs were followed by Sustainable Development Goals (SDGs), which echo human security principles through the focus on human protection (UN 2017).

On top of international bodies, several individual rich countries have gradually accepted that they have the obligation to promote human rights beyond their own territorial boundaries. They have also come to realize that they have a moral duty to help the poorest countries attain a sustainable economic development (Pratt 1999, p. 306). For example, Canada reshaped its foreign policy agenda to ensure that the country's International Development Agency (CIDA) was defined in humanitarian rather than commercial, political, or security terms since the 1970s (Pratt 1999, p. 307). Similarly, the concept of human security has been incorporated into the Japanese Foreign and Official Development Assistance policies since the 1990s to enable the country to proactively contribute to the world's peace and prosperity (Kitaoka 2016, p. 32).

Chapter 2

Key Human Security and Development Problems in Kenya

This chapter contains the most relevant literature and accounts from Kenyan citizens and residents who freely expressed their perspectives on the key domestic human security and development issues. As Jon Barnett and W. Neil Adger (2007, p. 642) acknowledge, there are numerous social determinants that are directly associated with human security and development. Although it may be impossible to cover all of them, this chapter identifies the main and the most complex ones in the local Kenyan and East African contexts, such as the impact of poverty, violent conflict and political intolerance, the growing terrorist threats, crimes, cultural beliefs and practices, and contemporary gender inequality involving sexual and gender-based violence (SGBV). The first and one of the most damaging is the high level of poverty, which adversely affects the overall productivity, including in the critical sectors of food security and climate change.

POVERTY, CLIMATE CHANGE, AND FOOD INSECURITY

Poverty and food insecurity are twin problems, as demonstrated by Alice Atieno Oluoko-Odingo (2011, p. 2), who makes a point that efforts to eradicate poverty usually have positive impacts on food and general human security. That point is also supported by Stephens et al. (2012, p. 424), who argue that poor agricultural production in Kenya comes with dire consequences, forcing the government and NGOs to prioritize initiatives and policies designed to improve food production. However, Stephens et al. further argue, there are always challenges. For example, Kenyan on-farm investments are highly dependent on the land's fertility, and therefore, farmers owning highly degraded soil refrain from heavily investing in fertilizers as it does not make a reasonable financial difference. Consequently, residents continue to experience failing yields and poverty, plunging into chronic food insecurity even with the availability of NGO- and government-funded programs (Stephens et al. 2012, p. 424). Accounts from my participants suggest that Oluoko-Odingo and Stephens et al. were correct, with Interviewee (31) arguing that poverty is the main threat to food production in the Western Province, his home region, as he puts it:

> Poverty is an issue. For example, some people have land, but they are unable to make use of it. They cannot afford fertilisers to put in the maize farm and therefore, they sow the maize just like that. That kind maize cannot generate profits. That alone can lead to poverty and hunger in the Western [province]. (Interviewee 31, male, foreign-aid beneficiary)

Through my many conversations with rural and remote Kenyans, it also came to my attention that the poorest Kenyan couples usually have the highest fertility rates. Consequently, even if foreign aid targeted agriculture to support small-scale farmers, it wouldn't lead to meaningful change because, on top of issues of soil fertility comes the problem with small land available to the large and poor families in the Kenyan society. While most Kenyans with whom I interacted undoubtedly understand that family planning can contribute to the betterment of maternal and child health, poor families still face a range of barriers, including poverty, that prevent them from fully accessing the relevant planning methods. As such, they continue making children, as my Interviewee (30) attests:

> In my area, we also have problems with land [. . .]. We have a small land available, while everyone keeps making children. They make too many children. (Interviewee 30, male, taxi driver)

Kenyans have been attempting to reduce poverty through economic growth, sustainable employment, and the provision of vital social services since the dawn of independence. Despite such great efforts, the results are disappointing for most. More than half of the Kenyan population is poor, with women and rural residents particularly vulnerable (Kristjanson et al. 2010, p. 979). Hundreds of thousands of young Kenyans do not find work, while around 85 percent of those who engage in paid work are employed in the informal sector (Lau et al. 2018, p. 1061). The high rates of unemployment and underemployment continue to affect the country despite a range of initiatives designed to alleviate poverty and the economic growth of 5 percent of the past few years (Business World Disrupt 2018). Poverty in Kenya affects most sectors, including food security, education, child safety, health, well-being, and housing. This is because, even with registered 11.6 percent growth in Kenyan national income per capita in 2021, for example, the amount remained low at USD1,979 (Mwaniki 2022). With such weak purchasing powers, it remains difficult for many Kenyans to afford even the basics, as attested by my Interviewee (21), who suggested that, with the cost of living in terms of rent and food, not everyone can afford the same things . . . people [in Kenya] are struggling to buy even a tomato (Interviewee 21, female, expatriate).

The point made by my Interviewee (22) aligns with the current literature. An assessment of food insecurity in Sub-Saharan Africa by the Food and Agriculture Organization (FAO) of the United Nations (2016) revealed that around 153 million individuals, that is, roughly 26 percent of the population aged above 15 years, suffered from severe food insecurity in the period between 2014 and 2015. In Kenya alone, 2.7 million individuals were classified as severely impacted by food insecurity in the first quarter of 2017 (FAO 2017). This was mainly due to three consecutive years of poor food production, exhausting people's coping capabilities, especially in the country's northeast, east, and coastal areas (FAO 2017).

On the other hand, Ochieng, Kirimi, and Makau (2016, p. 195) say that Kenyan farmers face the risks associated with climate change, a phenomenon that has significantly impacted their rain-fed agriculture, with smallholder farmers at the highest risk as they are forced to make decisions in a highly uncertain environment in relation to both rainfall and temperatures. Ochieng, Kirimi and Makau (2016, p. 195) further suggest that the consequences of climate change in Kenya have manifested themselves in different ways: soil erosion, flooding, landslides, warming, and droughts, all of which have led to soil degradation, impeding general food production, and worsening human security in turn. Evidence from my sample suggests that FAO's assessment and the points made by Ochieng, Kirimi, and Makau were correct. Interviewee (1) makes a point that the Kenyan rain patterns have changed, negatively impacting food production.

> The rains patterns have changed and that, in my view, affects food productivity. And of course, this is associated with different issues, including the high levels of deforestation. I think [that in] Kenya, as country, we are doing very poorly in terms of preserving our forest cover. (Interviewee 1, male, civil society activist and economist)

Enhancing disaster resilience in Kenya for stronger and safer communities remains critical. However, evidence suggests the Government of Kenya has failed to improve its capabilities to deal with climate change-induced natural disasters. The Kenyan government has further failed to adequately help build resilient communities and infrastructures to maximize preparedness to natural catastrophes, including droughts and flood emergencies, leading to serious consequences for food security (King-Okumu et al. 2018, p. 675). This literature was largely supported by my sample, such as my Interviewee (22), an NGO executive, who blames the Kenyan government for failing to coordinate actions designed to improve the resilience of Kenyan communities and effectively facilitate locally led recovery after flooding events. He gives an example:

> Last year, the weather forecast was pretty precise for the first time in my life. They warned people it is [was] going to rain like this. . . . It will cause floods in these areas, which are flood-prone areas. The government did not do anything until it started raining. (Interviewee 22, male, NGO's executive)

Climate change and food insecurity disproportionately affect poor people because poverty limits freedom of choice and access to opportunities that are vital for individuals' empowerment and safety (Njoya & Seetaram 2018, p. 513). Such material freedom enables citizens to reasonably choose the type of life they want and how to live it (Njoya & Seetaram 2018, p. 513). For poverty is not only about the lack of adequate household income but also the general capacity deprivation (Njoya & Seetaram 2018, p. 513). Unfortunately for poor countries, there are individuals who work hard, churning between low-paid and insecure employments, but never truly move away from poverty (Shildrick & MacDonald 2013, p. 286). From Kenyans' accounts, it can be established that, even with foreign-aid funds, poverty in the country is difficult to solve because it entails contradictory and changing requirements that are often difficult to recognize. With these findings and literature, it can be assumed that it will take a society with a high level of education and human capital to reverse these trends, which Kenyans do not generally possess.

POVERTY AND EDUCATION CHALLENGES

Poverty is a major hindrance for Kenyans to attain optimal education, which leads to a chain of other challenges and adversely affects the effectiveness of foreign aid. Vimefall, Andrén and Levin (2017, p. 81) make a point that the world has promoted children's access to primary education since the 1950s. Yet around one million Kenyan primary school-age children were not enrolled as per 2011. Furthermore, a report commissioned by UNICEF (2018) indicates that the proportion of out-of-school children at primary school level in Kenya was estimated at 15 percent, while the net attendance ratio in secondary school education was estimated at 59 percent in 2014.

Poor school enrollments come with dire consequences as there is a negative relationship between the quality of education attained by the general population and the level of poverty in society. Likewise, there is a positive relationship between the wages allocated to individuals and their level of education (Maiyo 2015, p. 142). This is relevant in the Kenyan context where, according to Abd Elrhman Elzahi Saaid Ali (2017, p. 2209), the population in the Kenyan North-East Province live in poorer conditions compared to residents of Nairobi and the Central Province because the North has been deprived of quality education. Similarly, participants in my research generally agree that people living in marginalized communities face rising unequal access to advantages, including education. For example, my Interviewee (39), a government official, suggests that people living in slums such as Kibera have less opportunities because their level of education is generally lower compared to the rest of Kenyan society. With so much poverty in the Kibera slum, school is not on the priority list, leading to a chain of other vulnerabilities.

Poverty challenges the ability to universally educate populations; that is, if parents are poor, their children are less likely to attend school. Conversely, the reduction of poverty through greater economic growth and improved health and well-being of the citizenry helps (Vimefall, Andrén & Levin 2017, p. 81). As Obeng-Odoom (2020, p. 137) puts it, such growth can only be achieved through education, which increases the supply of skilled workers. Obeng-Odoom's theory has been tested and confirmed by my sample, with my Interview (30) from the Luhya Community attesting that the longer it took communities to pursue educational post-colonialism, the harder it is to become competitive in the local labor market, as they claim below:

> In the Luhya land, it took a long time for people to know the value of education. So, when you get education late, it is hard to secure employment. They attempt to secure jobs, but they have no relevant qualification and certificates. (Interviewee 30, male, taxi driver)

The colonial education systems in Africa might have been designed and undertaken by separate entities, each with its own purpose, but it was never designed for the interests of the indigenous Africans. Well-established colonial systems and structures, Mwenda Ntarangwi (2003, p. 211) argues, imply that postcolonial Kenya could not reshape its educational system to tailor the content and pedagogy to the actual socio-economic and cultural realities on the ground. This argument is supported by Interviewee (56), who makes a point that poor quality education in Kenya has led to historical shortages in skills necessary to grow and sustain the local economy, adversely impacting the country's overall performance. He argues that indigenous Kenyans were not able to design a tertiary educational system that can generate strong and diversified skills that can help grow and sustain a domestic economy that can put Kenya in a position of strength in the global market and world order (Interviewee 56, male, Australian government official). That's why Abd Elrhman Elzahi Saaid Ali's (2017, p. 2209) suggestion that Kenya was ranked as 145 out of 186 countries in 2017, based on measures of standard of living, life expectancy, healthcare, and access to education, made total sense.

Glewwe, Kremer and Moulin (2009, p. 114) indicate that the challenge in Kenya is the high number of school dropouts due to poverty, on top of other vulnerabilities such as the conditions imposed by the Kenyan educational systems, with many schools promoting only clever students to grade eight and forcing the rest to repeat grade seven or drop out. In some regions, Glewwe, Kremer, and Moulin (2009, p. 114) further claim, many children quit school before they reach grade three. Accounts from my participants affirm Abd Elrhman Elzahi Saaid Ali and Glewwe, Kremer, and Moulin's points. Speaking from his lived experience, Interviewee (32) affirms that children from wealthy families are better off in terms of education because, in his own words, if you are in the group of those with nothing, your child misses out on education compared to the other group. For example, in Nairobi, some people have good businesses, and their children have access to good education. However, for others, even if you are employed, you are paid so little that it is not even enough to sustain the family. So, you end up in a situation where you are vulnerable (Interviewee 32, male, watchman).

A significant number of children in Sub-Saharan Africa also fall victim to harsh social realities such as the high prevalence of HIV/AIDS that kills their parents and destroys their support and funding sources. As per 2002, more than 15 million children had been orphaned by AIDS globally, and 12 million of these were Sub-Saharan Africans (Nyambedha & Aagaard-Hansen 2010, p. 555). By 1999, Kenya alone was home to around 860,000 AIDS orphans. Such conditions create a cycle between AIDS and poverty, with the affected families and their network progressively losing the means to support themselves because of the increasing numbers of orphaned children they suddenly must look after (Nyambedha & Aagaard-Hansen 2010, p. 555). My sample agrees, with Interviewee (8) making a point that becoming an orphan in Kenya means school dropout and a start of life on the street, as they put it:

> The mothers are dead—HIV [AIDS]. It's one of the causes leading to many orphans and, at times, they don't even have somewhere to go, or even the relatives reject them, or no one wants to take up [the] responsibility. (Interviewee 8, female, university student)

As demonstrated through the current literature and confirmed through Kenyans' accounts, poverty creates impoverishment in certain aspects of caregiving, compromising general child safety, which adversely affects vulnerable children's prospects for good education in turn. These conditions make it difficult for foreign aid to make a significant impact, particularly in Kenyan communities with deep-rooted child safety issues and intergenerational privation.

POVERTY AND CHILD SAFETY

Kenyan children in low-income families have their childhood compromised. UNICEF's 2017 situation analysis of children and women in Kenya suggests that around 3.6 million Kenyan children were classified as vulnerable (UNICEF 2017). Similarly, Kaime-Atterhög, Persson and Ahlberg (2017, p. 579) contend that children living on the street is common in poor and developing countries. These claims are also confirmed by M. Deghati's (2007) report, which indicates that there were between 250,000 and 300,000 street children in Kenya in 2007. Similarly, a more recent study by Florence Kanorio Kisirkoi and Godfrey Shed Mse (2016, p. 89) suggests that the streets of Nairobi alone were home to between 60,000 and 80,000 children in 2016. Kaime-Atterhög, Persson and Ahlberg (2017, p. 579) made a point that, despite the legislation and services to protect the rights of these children, Kenyan laws make no provisions for poor and dysfunctional families who are unable to provide vital care. Evidence from my sample supports this literature, with Interviewee (38) suggesting that some children are abandoned on the streets by their own hopeless parents because of the cycle of deprivation that affects their ability to break free from extreme poverty. He gives an example that someone might lie and say to you, "Can you please keep this child for me briefly?" But what you don't know is that they are leaving this child with you, just to run away from their responsibility to raise the child (Interviewee 38, male, primary school teacher).

Despite the system and society's marginalization, some street children work hard, sometimes with little earnings. However, most of them are hardened criminals (Mikulak 2003, p. 391). There is a range of social factors linked with this phenomenon. Most of the street children come from settlement communities plagued by alcohol, diseases, and extreme poverty (Mikulak 2003, p. 391). Such a level of poverty leads to counterproductive behaviors such as poor access to preventive health, failure, or unwillingness to adhere to drug regimens, bad working ethics, poor parenthood, and bad management of finances, all of which leads to families' total collapse (Mani et al. 2013, p. 976). That's why some Kenyan children have no choice but to leave their family homes simply because life at home is far worse than the conditions on the street, as Interviewee (23) explains:

> Chokora [derogatory Swahili word for "street children"] are there because they do not have enough food at their own homes, and the environment in their

> homes is not good at all. So, they have no choice, but to try luck out of home [. . .] Not every child on the street is an orphan. (Interviewee 23, male, security guard and foreign-aid beneficiary)

My first impression during my PhD data collection in Nairobi was that the literature got it all wrong. I could not see street children in Kilimani, a prestigious suburb where I lived. However, accounts from Nairobi residents familiar with the street children situation confirmed the points made by Deghati, Kisirkoi, and Mse, as well as Kaime-Atterhög, Persson, and Ahlberg. Interviewee (18), an NGO's senior staff familiar with the situation, suggests that street children are not present everywhere in Nairobi. "They agglomerate only in poverty-stricken suburbs. There, you would certainly find a lot of street children [. . .]. Slums basically, like Kibera," he confidently claims.

Once on the streets, street children engage in hard labor such as car washing, carrying loads of packages, shoe shining, collecting garbage for resale, wandering up and down and, most dangerously, stealing (Mikulak 2003, p. 391). They hardly maintain themselves financially as their income-generating activities are constantly disrupted by crises, including a cycle of violence and conflicts with the police, arrests, incarcerations, and illnesses (Auerswald et al. 2012, p. s5). That's why, my Interviewee (18) suggests, the city council officers chase street children and homeless people away from the city center without providing any durable solutions, as he claims:

> I know there have been a drive by the city council to get rid of a lot of these street kids and homeless [people]. I mean you still see a number of homeless people. You just prevent them from being there, like you just chase them away. It is not like you are actually providing a solution. It's like . . . basically cleaning up the city. (Interviewee 18, male, senior NGO's staff)

Embleton et al. (2018) say that street children live in precarious conditions as they try to generate income and fight for their survival. They are vulnerable to diseases and are highly marginalized. They face many human rights violations, which often lead to a disproportionate burden of morbidities, substance abuse, and mental problems (Embleton et al. 2018). Auerswald et al. (2012, p. s5) make a similar point that life on the streets leads to drug dealing and addiction because, with increasing hunger and loneliness, children on the streets are tempted to sniff glue to get high, hoping to relieve their misery. My sample affirms Auerswald et al.'s conclusions, as well as Embleton et al.'s points. Interviewee (46) is a young adult male who grew up living on the street in Nairobi. He is currently undergoing drug and alcohol rehabilitation at a center in Nairobi. Here, he describes life on the street as

> constant hardships—being beaten by the members of the public [. . .]. Just random people coming and bulling [hitting with head] you, even if you have done

> nothing wrong to that individual. That is one of the reasons why I prefer living here [at the rehab centre]. (Interviewee 46, male, former street child)

As William Githira, who as a 15-year-old boy lived on the street in Nairobi, said in 2007, nobody cares about street children, whether they live or die (cited in Deghati 2007). This literature is confirmed by my Interviewee (47), another young adult and former street child also undergoing rehabilitation at the same center as Interviewee (46), who suggests that life on the street can be unbearable. He gives an example:

> A friend of mine killed himself. [. . .] He was stealing wires from Kenya Power. He was cutting them with a hand saw and sold them. At some point, he was caught in the act and taken to Kilimani [police station, Nairobi]. They were to jail him. He was tired of life in jail [He had previously been arrested multiple times] and that's why he decided to kill himself. (Interviewee 47, male, former street child)

In places like Kisumu, newly arrived street children are taken into the so-called bases controlled by older youth. These older boys become bullies and often use the new street boys as "their girls," and that implies employing anal sex as a form of demonstration of power and domination (Auerswald et al. 2012, p. s5). For most street children, the commencement of life on the streets means the immediate start of sexual exploitation, with sexual acts involving children as young as five years old (Embleton et al. 2015, p. 4). Interviewee (49) explains that, for a girl to survive on the street, she must get married. She needs to have a man, that is, basically another street male child who can look after her, take care of her, and protect her from other street children. Otherwise, it would really get rough for her (Interviewee 49, female, NGO's staff, and former government official).

The number of people under the age of 18 for whom the street has become home and the main source of income continues to increase (Rončević, Stojadinović & Batrnekantonić 2013, p. 841), compromising the living conditions, health, and well-being of the marginalized poor. This is exacerbated by a social structure in countries like Kenya, where the health systems are not optimally organized by the government to meet citizens' existing complex demands.

POVERTY, HEALTH MANAGEMENT, AND GENERAL WELL-BEING

Kenya is one of the Sub-Saharan African countries with critical healthcare workforce shortages. The country has an average of 1.46 healthcare workers per 1,000 residents, compared with 2.5 healthcare workers per 1,000 people recommended by the World Health Organization (Njuguna, Mwangi & Kamau 2014, p. 204). While there have been some progresses in the health sector generally, any significant changes will depend on the systemic approach to health financing reform with a focus on equity and efficiency. Thus, most of the policies and initiatives designed to promote equity and address the needs of vulnerable populations have, so far, largely failed (Chuma & Okungu 2011, p. 1). Hence, despite the UN's Millennium Development Goals' (MDGs) objective to combat poverty, hunger, disease, and a range of other underlying factors of Kenyans' health and well-being, the country remained far from attaining these goals by their desired timeframe of 2015 (Kingery et al. 2016, p. 92). Evidence from my sample indicates that the above literature does not exaggerate when suggesting that policies and initiatives designed to promote equity have largely failed. Interviewee (49) makes a point that, while the quality of health services has improved in city settings, the situation is different in rural and remote areas.

> Health is also a big issue. Most of the cities or most of the towns, they have a hospital. Let me call it a district hospital that should have all the basic requirements in a hospital . . . they have tried to equip them very well. But, out of that town, going into the village, it is a different story. Not everybody can access the healthcare that they need. Women having to deliver [babies] . . . with midwives in the[ir] house or the traditional attendants. (Interviewee 49, female, NGO's staff, and former government official)

Maternal mortality rate in Kenya was estimated at 530 per 100,000 live births in 2008, while the under-five-year-old mortality rate was estimated at 84 per 1,000 in 2009 (Kingery et al. 2016, p. 92). According to the World Health Organization (2018), the leading causes of child mortality in Kenya are acute respiratory infections, birth asphyxia, prematurity, diarrhea, injuries, neonatal sepsis, congenital anomalies, and HIV/AIDS. Kenyan society is plagued with an increasing number of deadly diseases, putting more pressure on the already fragile health system (CDC 2018), with COVID-19 adding 96,139 infected cases and 1,665 deaths as per December 29, 2020 (Ministry of Health 2020). My Interviewee (28) agrees with the literature above and makes a point that you don't have to live remotely to experience health inequity in Kenya. People in poor neighborhoods are among the most vulnerable as well. She explains:

> Health problem is something else that is affecting those who are in the slums. Even me, myself, because the government isn't doing enough. We are doing NHI (National Hospital Insurance Fund), but every time you pop into the hospital, no drugs. And that is a national disaster. (Interviewee 28, male, NGO's frontline staff)

The world recorded approximately 219 million malaria cases and 435,000 deaths in 2017. About 92 percent of these were recorded in the Sub-Saharan African region, with children under the age of five accounting for 61 percent of all malaria casualties. Approximately 70 percent of Kenyans live in malaria-prone areas, and the country is on the top 15 malaria list. The disease is the second biggest killer, accounting for around 8 percent of mortality incidences (Gopal et al. 2019, p. 2). Were et al. (2018) argue that the level and severity of malaria and other diseases in Kenya were directly linked to health expenditure and households' financial status, and therefore, remarkable health inequalities were observed in rural and remote areas. My sample makes a similar point, with Interviewee (30) claiming that a limited number of Kenyans can afford medical costs.

> In Kenya, a lot of people are poor [. . .]. It is hard in terms of health and well-being. Many poor people die due to their inability to cover medical expenses . . . healthcare is very expensive. Because even if you go to the government hospital, you will need to buy medicines. These medicines are very expensive. (Interviewee 30, male, taxi driver)

Winter, Dzombo, and Barchi (2019) argue that housing is a significant social determinant of health. This is evident in the Kenyan context where it has been proven that the well-being of residents in the slums is compromised due to their living conditions, with poor housing, water, and sanitation. The overcrowding, coupled with the lack of proper waste management, increases residents' risk of consumption of unsafe water and direct exposure to human feces (Winter, Dzombo & Barchi 2019). Speaking from lived experience, my sample affirms this literature, indicating that overcrowding in the slums makes it easier for infectious diseases to spread quickly:

> Obviously, when you are living in a small place [with] so many people, when there is an outbreak of a disease, it spreads very fast. That . . . is an obvious thing and that one happens a lot when you are growing up. For example, if you look at my skin, you know that I had a skin disease growing up. . . also chicken pox. (Interviewee 4, male, government official and former NGO's frontline staff)

Poor housing and poor infrastructure have become a major hindrance to attaining an acceptable standard of health and well-being in Kenya, particularly in poor neighborhoods such as the slums. The general lack of critical facilities in Kibera, for example, implies that some people do not have access to toilets. They help themselves in plastic bags at night, which they subsequently throw away in the morning, hence the local concept of the *flying toilet*. Alarmingly, the endless piles of rubbish in Kibera's streets sometimes contain human feces. Interviewee (31) explains its implication:

> These flying toilets is about people who help themselves in plastic bags and they throw it away in the night. Whether it lands on another person's roof, they don't care [. . .]. The main effect of it is the cholera. (Interviewee 31, male, foreign-aid beneficiary)

All the examples above demonstrate how poverty adversely shapes Kenyan health services and housing, which affects the citizens' well-being in turn. As Interviewee (38) rightfully puts it, hungry people are angry people, and that makes it easier for Kenyan politicians to steer vulnerable populations into politically motivated violent conflicts.

VIOLENT CONFLICTS AND POLITICAL INTOLERANCE

Kenyan society has long been characterized both by political and tribal violence, especially since the implementation of a multiparty democratic system in the 1990s (Wanjiru 2018, p. 1) because of excessive manipulations by political elites. Four major incidents of electoral violence were registered in Kenya in 1991, 1993, 1997, and 2007. These incidents were strategically planned by political actors to instigate fear, harm, blackmail, and abuse, targeting political actors in ways that influenced the electoral processes and election outcomes (Muhammad, D'Souza & Amponsah 2013, p. 20). Similarly, Taylor, Pevehouse, and Straus (2017, p. 398) suggest that, in the 1990s' events and other incidents of the same nature, violence was used as a strategy to influence election outcomes because domestic democratic institutions were immature and weak. They argue that violence forces the opposition to boycott the elections, effectively paving the way for an incumbent's easy victory. Evidence from my sample indicates that these authors were correct, with Interviewee (38) suggesting that the Kenyan populace can be easily manipulated, thus making it easier for politicians to use them for their own political ends because average citizens, grassroots people never understand the concept of democracy. They are overloaded with too much information. Most importantly, they just follow a person, a political leader and political agenda they do not really understand (Interviewee 38, male, primary school teacher).

Even local Kenyan authorities, including mayors, police chiefs, and village executives, promote electoral violence for their own self-survival reasons (Hassan & O'Mealia 2018, p. 161). They possess great knowledge of the local communities, and their positions provide them with coercive and overwhelming powers over their subjects (Hassan & O'Mealia 2018, p. 161). On the other hand, Obala and Mattingly (2014, p. 2735) argue that there is a correlation between tribalism, corruption, and violence. Tribalism fuels the historical land conflicts in Kenya while corruption enhances them, resulting in perpetual violent clashes, and this has been attested by my Interviewee (28) who suggests that politics alone does not lead to violence in Kenya. It is a combination of politics, tribalism, and corruption—in his own words, "the three Kenyan monsters," as he claims:

> I see three things: politics, then tribalism and corruption [. . .]. I think politics is [. . .] a part of us, Kenyans. Politics divide us . . . and when the politics is divided, we do the ethnicity—we group us according to our tribes, and the third thing is corruption. If those three things are dealt with, I think anything else can be done [. . .]. Those three monsters. (Interviewee 28, male, NGO's frontline staff)

The contentious rhetoric around the land issue has always been a great tool for politicians to organize violence and to attract ordinary Kenyans to participate (Klaus 2017, p. 52). Such narratives played a major role in electoral violence in the 1990s as well as during the 2007–2008 post-election violent clashes (Klaus 2017, p. 52). This is because, Kathleen Klaus (2017, p. 52) argues, candidates and political elites use specific rhetoric to convince voters that their access to the land depends on the election outcomes, sparking fears or hopes, especially where average, poor Kenyans can preempt their eviction by rivals. Tribal and ethnic conflicts have historically led to a cycle of violence and a war of all-against-all, particularly between the major, politically minded ethnic groups. It all starts as a normal political campaign but, at some point, turns into a struggle between the alliance of Luo and Kalenjin against the Kikuyu people (Somerville 2011, p. 82). Othering and unfair distribution of Kenyan wealth means that a large part of society, especially electorates supporting the opposition, misses out. This obvious unfairness creates tensions and anger, as Interviewee (38) explains:

> In terms of [political] intolerance, it often occurs when tribalism is involved. When they start saying the "other" is in power, and those who are in power only care about their own people. It is not done in a way that everyone is represented. So, hungry people are angry people. Those who miss out are angry and sometimes, it triggers revolts, but often based on ethnicity. (Interviewee 38, male, primary school teacher)

On the other hand, the local Kenyan media also plays a big role in these violent conflicts. For example, the 2007 post-election violence was aggravated by the inter-ethnic hatred inflicted by media propaganda, particularly that of vernacular radio stations, which broadcast hateful rhetoric and key messages directly to the conflicting parties (Somerville 2011, p. 82). Such radical media coverages have intensified tribal tensions in some parts of Kenya, especially in the North, to a point where targeting some groups in the community is viewed as morally correct, natural, and traditional (Carrier & Kochore 2014, p. 138). Similarly, political candidates and political elites use specific rhetoric to convince voters that their access to core resources depends on the election outcomes, sparking fears or hopes, especially where average, poor Kenyans can preempt their eviction by rivals (Carrier & Kochore 2014, p. 138). Interviewee (41) fully agrees.

> Every time you have elections, you have opportunities [risks] for violence, and I think it is largely hinged upon the insecurities that arise from the fact that people do not have their very basics [basic needs] met. The majority of the people do not have this. (Voice 041, male, Catholic priest and academic)

Kenyan political candidates' adoption of violent rhetoric of exclusion to gain the vote of those who radically oppose certain community groups enforces their newly established presumption that only some groups in the Kenyan community are morally correct, natural, and traditional, causing further security challenges in a country already facing very serious terrorist threats.

TERRORIST THREATS

Kenya has been a hotbed of terrorism for a very long time, and its vulnerability to terrorist attacks partially stems from its proximity to Somalia (Tharoor 2015). For example, the 1998 bombing of the U.S. Embassy in Nairobi by Somali militants caused more than 200 deaths and around 5,000 injuries (Cooke 2018). Similarly, the UN reports (as cited in Wallis 2003) established that an Al-Qaeda cell was responsible for the 2002 bombing of a tourist hotel on the Kenyan coast, killing 15 people and using Somalia as a base for training, supply, and cover. Verbal evidence from my sample affirms these reports when Interviewee (36) argues that Kenya's overall security depends on Somalia's stability. As he puts it:

> Kenya, being a neighbour of Somalia, yes, they do have that threat until the Somali Al-Shabaab is defeated. Until the stability, peace . . . is promoted in Somalia and then, they will be good neighbours. And promote each other[s] . . . economic integration, political interaction. (Interviewee 36, male, Catholic priest, and NGO's executive)

In September 2013, a major terror attack was carried out at the Westgate Mall where terrorists held a four-day siege that caused 67 fatalities and 175 injuries (Simon et al. 2014, p. e104136), and Al-Shabaab claimed responsibility for the attack (BBC 2013). As recently as January 2019, five heavily armed Al-Shabaab militants stormed Nairobi's DusitD2 Hotel, killing 21 and injuring 28 people (BBC 2019b). Several attacks have been planned or carried out by Al-Shabaab using improvised explosive devices (IEDs) in recent years, particularly in the districts of Mandera, Wajir, Garissa, and Dadaab, all of which are geographically located in Northern Kenya (Xinhua News Agency 2017). In June 2017, at least four people were killed after a car they occupied ran over an explosive device at the northern border town of Kulan in the Garissa district (Hajir 2017). Interviewee (29) endorses this literature, arguing that it is easier for Somali terrorists to penetrate Kenya because the Kenyan Somalians at the border towns in Kenya behave, sound, and look like Somalians on the other side in Somalia. Therefore, it is easy to penetrate and infiltrate and harder for Kenyan authorities to control migration between the two countries, largely compromising border and overall security (Interviewee 29, male, lieutenant general in the army). Interviewee (31) holds the same view as Interviewee (29), and he is anxious about the Somalians' presence in Kenya, especially in Nairobi. He argues that it is practically impossible to effectively protect Kenyan borders simply because Somalians on both sides have the same physical features, as he puts it:

> Woria [a derogatory name for Somali people], they are so many here. When they arrive here in Kenya, you cannot tell who is who [anymore]. You can't tell. There are Woria from Kenya, and there are Woria from Somalia. So, when they are mixed, you can no longer tell who is Woria from Kenya. (Interviewee 31, male, foreign-aid beneficiary)

In 2013, a BBC report suggested that Al-Shabaab's increasing attacks on Kenya were a response to Kenyan military involvement in Somalia, a point supported by Interviewee (43), who suggests that Kenyan involvement in the fight against terrorists in Somalia might have intensified these attacks, and they put it:

> Understandably, Al-Shabaab makes it clear [. . .]. They threaten saying, "If you do not remove your soldiers here, we will be attacking you, on your soil in Kenya." That is why this is the most threatened country in the region. (Interviewee 43, male, colonel in the army)

The point made by Interviewee 43 makes political and international relations sense, but it is not convincing. Even if Kenya were not involved in the fight against Al-Shabaab, terrorists would still have other targets in and outside Somalia. For example, master minders often specifically target school children to demonstrate Al-Shabaab's opposition to Western-style educational systems (Xinhua News Agency 2017). Therefore, Interviewee (18) was right to argue that Somali-based terrorists would attack Kenya, especially in Nairobi, regardless of their involvement in the Somali war. The reason being that if Al-Shabaab wants to hit the Americans and the British hard, which is a top priority for global terrorists, Kenya is a great place to start (Interviewee 18, male, senior NGO's staff). Interviewee (45) agrees with Interviewee's (18) claims, arguing that Islamism is the issue, not necessarily a revenge on the Kenyan involvement in Somalia. Terrorist groups have launched several deadly attacks in Kenya over the last few years, targeting Christian-dominated schools, including the April 2015 attack in Northern Kenya by Al-Shabaab, brutally massacring 147 students from Garissa University (CNN 2015). Rhetorically, my Interviewee (45) questions:

> why don't they revenge by attacking [Kenyan] mosques? They usually target churches, or streets where they are sure there are not many Muslims there. However, if there is a mosque in the neighbourhood or there are Muslims, there will not be explosions [. . .]. There was [the] day a bus was hijacked at Mandera [North Kenya, border to Somalia]. You were required to read the Koran to survive. They formed a queue. Even if you had memorised one line of Koran, that was enough to save you. (Interviewee 45, female, housekeeper)

The points above indicate that Joanna Bar (2016, p. 148) was right to argue that Islamic terrorism continues to affect Kenya's security in various ways. It causes deaths and spreads violence across borders, becoming a major challenge to Kenya's foreign policy. These points are further supported by Interviewee (29), who suggests that Al-Shabaab is a regional and global security threat. He explains that Al-Shabaab is a terrorist group with solid links to Al-Qaeda. It is also a part of a well-established and elaborated international terrorist system. For that reason, it is now trying to spread beyond Somalia, to many places—Kenya, Tanzania . . . everywhere. They have even mentioned attacking Burundi because of the soldiers from there in Somalia. In fact, if one country faces terror threats, it affects the rest of the countries in the East African Community (Interviewee 29, male, lieutenant general in the army). But there are terrorists from within Kenya too. Such new developments test the country's ability to deal with internally and externally driven extremism. Interviewee (7) puts it this way:

> There is also the aspect of depression that is happening. Of late, we've had quite a number of young people committing suicide [attacks] because of a lot of stress

> on us [. . .]. The lack of employment becomes a challenge to security and peace and of course that also results . . . [in] extremism that we are encountering in Kenya right now because people are taking the religion as a form of advocating for their own ideals. And of course, if you look at it, sometimes it is not a matter of religion . . . they are being paid to be part of these groups. So, it is an easy way to make money. (Interviewee 7, female, NGO's executive)

Terrorism continues to adversely impact Kenyan human security. More alarmingly, Kenyan-born terrorists are being paid and doing the bidding of terrorist leaders because they live in abject poverty. If East African governments do not improve their citizens' general living conditions, the situation will continue to deteriorate, particularly with the continuous rise of other major challenges such as the high level of crime.

THE IMPACTS OF CRIMES

The high level of crime in Kenya adversely affects citizens and residents' health, well-being, and general safety. Kennedy A. Mkutu and Kizito Sabala (2007, p. 391) argue that optimal security in any given country depends on the state's ability to guarantee its citizens' welfare by providing them with adequate property and physical security guarantees. This is not the case in Kenya where, for example, *The Economist* (2002, p. 50) reports that crimes are historically under-reported, and yet, the police data indicate a high level of crimes such as mugging, a crime that has progressively become common in places like Nairobi, making the capital city dangerous and often lawless. Accounts from my participants suggest that *The Economist* report and Mkutu and Sabala's findings about safety in Nairobi were accurate. Interviewee (18) has lived, studied, and worked in Nairobi for several years. He argues that there are many safe cities where millennials would feel comfortable in Africa, but Nairobi is not one of them. Asked to elaborate further on his security and safety assessment in Nairobi, he claims:

> . . . There is that general sense that this is not a city you can walk anywhere you want. There are some cities in Africa, one I would point [to is] Kigali [Capital City of Rwanda] for instance or Addis [Ababa, Ethiopia] where people most of the time feel safe to walk at night in most places. Nairobi is not such a city. (Interviewee 18, male, Senior NGO's staff)

Violent crimes in Kenya are also widespread in other major tourist cities such as Mombasa (Business Monitor International 2018). While it is broadly acknowledged that the situation has recently improved, the Kenyan Police

Force remains ineffective in their dealing with crimes mainly due to corruption and the lack of appropriate resources (Business Monitor International 2018). Interviewee (55), a Kenyan citizen and former resident of Nairobi, suggests that some Kenyan towns have progressively become so dangerous that you can now only go around its Central Business District (CBD) if you must, as she puts it:

> Mugging is a very common [crime], especially if you go to [the] CBD. So, if you don't need to go to the CBD, you just completely avoid it. (Interviewee 55, female, lawyer)

Random attacks can occur anywhere in Kenya, including places that once were culturally and religiously holy such as convents. They also involve terrible actions, making it difficult for victims to get over the trauma generated by these experiences (Halpern 2011, p. 54). The offenders often threaten their victims with rape and point guns at their heads in desperate attempts to force them to reveal where they hide their money. Some victims cannot handle so much pressure—they weep, scream, and sometimes collapse helplessly (Halpern 2011, p. 54). While boys of all ages have more exposure to assaultive violence involving robbing, mugging, beating, and sexual assaults than girls in town settings (Seedat et al. 2004, p. 173), robbery has dire impacts on all population groups regardless of a person's gender or age in the countryside and remote areas (Mugambi & Mbuba 2011, p. 6). This is because the only wealth that can be stolen from the Kenyan countryside is livestock, including herds of cattle, goats, and sheep, all of which are the main investment and main source of income. In other words, livestock is the only means for survival for the people in this part of the world and losing it means the destruction of life, a big blow for the owners and their family. Therefore, concerned countrymen will do whatever it takes, including using machine guns, to protect this valuable property (Mugambi & Mbuba 2011, p. 6). But they also use the same guns to steal from others, as Interviewee (25) attests from his experience in Turkana, northwest Kenya:

> Other crimes are linked to robbery—cattle rustling. Usually, Turkana [people] possess machine guns. Therefore, sometimes they use them for their own security, but some of them use these for cattle rustling in other areas. Due to the hardships they face, some of them are left with no choice, but to become robbers. They usually steal the cattle. (Interviewee 25, male, foreign-aid beneficiary, and NGO's frontline staff)

Crimes, including murders, in Kenya affect locals and foreign nationals almost equally. For example, Gabrielle Maina, an Australian teacher who had been residing and working in one of the prestigious schools in Nairobi, was shot dead by assailants on motorbikes in a botched robbery in 2017 (Duffin & Higgins 2017). Earlier in 2013, the Australian Department of Foreign Affairs confirmed they were providing consular assistance to the family of Patrick John Richer, an Australian citizen who was shot dead in Kenya (Masuku 2013). The local news and police authorities reported at the time that at least 10 armed attackers raided Patrick's house and shot him twice in the chest at close range (Masuku 2013). Much earlier, in 2008, Graham Warren, a 58-year-old Briton, was murdered in a bungled robbery in front of his wife when he attempted to resist thieves who had broken into his family home in Watamu, a small coastal city, stealing 6,000 Pounds (Crilly 2008). In 2007, Julian Nathan, a citizen of New Zealand who lived and worked in Kenya for an Australasian avocado oil company, was attacked by five men at his home, bashing him to death before fleeing the crime scene with a significant but undisclosed amount of money (The Advertiser 2007). This literature has been confirmed by some of my participants, with Interviewee (25) going a bit further to explain how the Kenyan society's attitude toward crimes in conjunction with the high level of impunity creates a haven for criminals.

> Look, in Kakuma [Northwest Kenya], you can be arrested for a crime as serious as a murder or threatening people in the open daylight. You can also be arrested for raping a very small child. However, most of these criminals are out of custody within three days. So, you understand that impunity makes criminals feel comfortable. They face no consequences. And I am sure the same thing is happening in the rest of the country. (Interviewee 25, male, foreign-aid beneficiary, and NGO's frontline staff)

The level, intensity, and frequency of crimes prevent international investors from readily engaging in Kenyan business activity—too risky. This avoidance causes big losses to the Kenyan economy and hence negatively affects general human security; that is, poverty rates continue to grow as a result (Business Monitor International 2018). At the same time, this same insecurity makes it expensive to do business in Kenya as investors are left with no choice but to hire private security guards (Business Monitor International 2018). Interviewee (15), a small business owner in a poor neighborhood in Nairobi, affirms Business Monitor International's findings that insecurity makes doing business in Kenya too risky.

> There are some people who do their business at a place called Kawangwale [. . .]. Last time I spoke to them, they had come to their store and found it empty. When I asked them if they had left the shop unlocked, they said they had locked it. Things seemed normal, but they noticed they failed to tighten one lock. That is what enabled the thief to easily break and enter. [. . .] The consequence is

> our inability to catch up again [and] accumulate [. . .] capital. (Interviewee 15, female, small business owner and NGO's frontline staff)

Jerome Starkey (2013, p. 45) makes a point that ransom-related kidnappings are common, putting the lives of Kenyan residents and visitors, especially those of Western complexion, at high security risk. Similar conclusions were drawn by Business Monitor International (2018), suggesting that violent crimes in Kenya are particularly widespread in major tourist cities such as Mombasa and Nairobi. Evidence from my sample suggests that these reports are correct, with Interviewee (12) claiming that when Kenyans see a foreigner, they see cash, which is probably relatively true but unfortunate for the immediate health and welfare of Westerners. She said to me: "I told you; Kenyans think all foreigners have money—when they see you, they see money" (Interviewee 12, female, private business director). The literature and findings in this section consist of just a few examples of how the level and complexities in crimes affect human security and foreign-aid effectiveness in Kenya, a society where, on top of poverty, most of the social determinants of health and well-being are amplified by cultural beliefs and practices.

CULTURAL BELIEFS AND PRACTICES

Some Kenyan beliefs and cultural practices put some members of the community in vulnerable positions. They are also detrimental to the effectiveness of foreign aid. How? Hamisi Mathias Machangu (2015, p. 274) writes that many Africans believe in magical powers that can be used to turn a human into an animal, call up the spirit of a dead person, diagnose and cure illnesses, or cause diseases in other humans, misfortunes, or sudden deaths. Kenyans believe that poor older people, especially women, usually have magic powers. As such, they are often targeted for murder or forced to relocate from their traditional homes due to the community's suspicion that they are witches (Machangu 2015, p. 275). Miranda Forsyth (2016, p. 335) makes a similar point that anyone in African societies, including men, women, poor, and rich, can become a victim of witchcraft accusations. However, elderly women, especially those with unusual physical appearances, are at the highest risk. That is why Forsyth (2016, p. 336) suggests, the elderly, isolated members of society, and the disabled usually face a wave of violence as the rest of the community believes that, with their physical differences, they must be witches.

On the other hand, a significant number of Africans understand that witchcraft implies supernatural techniques for good or bad, and such understanding fosters fear of bewitchment and promotes witchcraft accusations, entailing severe sanctions such as social isolation, destruction of property, and ritual killings, all of which continue to impede the general human security of the victims, their families, and society (Gershman 2016, p. 182). Accounts from my Kenyan sample suggest that these reports are correct in that cultural beliefs and practices put some Kenyan citizens at risk. Interviewee (31), a Kenyan citizen who holds firsthand knowledge about witchcraft killings, confirms that they are a common occurrence in his home district of Kisii.

> That happens in Kisii. There is, for example, a time where they were killed. They were burnt alive. There were around ten of them. They were pretending to be traditional healers, but actually, they were witches. (Interviewee 31, male, foreign-aid beneficiary)

An Al Jazeera report (2009) also confirms the point made by Interviewee (31) on the commonness of witchcraft killings in Kisii, a community where the use of magic power to harm is largely believed, putting the elderly at risk of mob attacks and killings. More alarmingly, Odhiambo Joseph (2009) writes, people, including local authorities, usually do not protest or attempt to stop witchcraft killings because the young men who carry out these killings are convinced that witches deserve death. As such, these killings are difficult to curb because the offenders usually get away with it, thus enhancing the culture of impunity. Interviewee (33) explains that victims are attacked by the entire community, and authorities are unable or unwilling to find out who exactly committed the atrocities against those who are suspected of being witches. As such, for their records, authorities, including the police, just note the incident as "a mob attack," and this implies that there is no follow-up because, normally, there is no suspect in the case. Victims are burned by "the mob." But who is the mob? The question remains a mystery for many cases (Interviewee 33, female, NGO's frontline staff).

But Kenya is also home to a great number of traditional healers. Rebecca Gearhart and Munib Said Abdulrehman (2014, p. 219) write that there are members of the community who trust traditional healers more than the official health systems. Community members turn to traditional healers for different physical, mental, or spiritual issues, adversely affecting modern medicine adherence and the patient's recovery. Mshana et al. (2006, p. 46) came to the same conclusions, arguing that patients in Sub-Saharan Africa sometimes opt for wrong interventions simply because they believe the causes of a given medical condition are witchcraft. My sample strongly agrees. Interviewee (10) gives a typical example from the Kenyan context where HIV was initially thought of as witchcraft, not necessarily a sexually transmitted disease, because many people didn't understand it. Some people in the community strongly believed that young girls who were virgins would be a treatment; that is, having sexual intercourse with a virgin helps cure HIV/AIDS. So, a lot of young girls, school-age girls, also contracted the disease at that time because most men thought they were a solution to their problem (Interview 10, female, academic and former official in the Kenyan department of foreign affairs).

Such accounts suggest it is difficult for any initiatives, including foreign-aid projects, to make a significant impact due to Kenyans' cultural understanding and mindset. For example, some Kenyans turn to dishonest traditional healers for a range of medical conditions first and foremost, and some of these healers go as far as pretending to have what it takes to cure HIV/AIDS. In his own words, Interviewee (31) explains that "[healers] would do anything possible. Some people have gone so far and promised to cure HIV/AIDS, despite the fact we know it is hard to get rid of HIV/AIDS" (Interviewee 30, male, taxi driver). Besides, some practices by Kenyan traditional healers are robbery. Interviewee (31) further explains:

> It is a problem for the Kenyan society. Some of these [healers] are not trustworthy. Some will require up to 200,000 [Kenyan Shillings, approximately USD2,000]. You give them this money, but your problems keep increasing [. . .]. This is particularly problematic for businessmen with money. They are scammed by these traditional doctors saying, "If you want more money, give me so much and I will make it happen." They are just scammed [. . .]. Poor people are scammed for 500 Kenyan shillings, 1000 Kenyan shillings. (Interviewee 31, male, foreign-aid beneficiary)

Besides, practices that might be outdated or immoral by Western standards, such as widow inheritance, continue to affect Kenyans' health and well-being, increasing the prevalence of HIV/AIDS in females (Agot et al. 2010, p. e14028). Polygamy also shapes the fate of Kenyan females, particularly in regions that have not attained an optimal level of education (Fenske 2015, p. 60). Interviewee (10), a Luo, confirms the high prevalence of polygamy in her culture and explains that it usually happens when a husband dies, with his brother culturally expected to inherit the widow as his new wife. So, it is a legit affair, and everyone knows; it's not wrong in the eyes of the community—it is morally correct (Interview 10, female, academic and former official in the Kenyan department of foreign affairs). These findings and literature on cultural beliefs and practices pinpoint complexities in the African practices and the need for mindset changes. This is particularly true in the following important areas of gender inequality and sexual- and gender-based violence.

CONTEMPORARY GENDER INEQUALITY AND SEXUAL- AND GENDER-BASED VIOLENCE

There is a significant gender imbalance in Kenyan society, which limits the effectiveness of foreign aid. For example, Kenyan men generally possess higher human capital and skills, which leads to a justified gender pay gap (Agesa, Agesa & Dabalen 2009, p. 431). This aligns with Sarah Jewitt and Harriet Ryley's (2014, p. 137) point that women generally face barriers as they try to attain education and subsequently meaningful employment in Sub-Saharan Africa. These barriers include early pregnancies, violence, and sexually transmitted diseases. My participants affirm the points these authors made, with Interviewee (25) suggesting that poor education in Kenyan women is one of the main reasons why they are oppressed. Worse again, Interviewee (25) further claims, there are no tangible initiatives being implemented to rectify such negative trends. For girls' education to be promoted, Interviewee (25) suggests, at least one family member must have an understanding so that they can promote the importance of education for the Kenyan female population (Interviewee 25, male, foreign-aid beneficiary, and NGO's frontline staff). Interviewee (19) agrees that gender inequality is a reality in Sub-Saharan Africa and suggests that the promotion of the feminist agenda is not an easy task. Even though she herself is an educated nun, consistent with Catholic Church teachings, she does not believe men and women should be equal, and this belief is deep-rooted in Kenyan society, as she puts it:

> We can never be equal. A man can never be equal, a woman in the same [sense]. It is vice-versa in the sense of the way one is created . . . biologically. We can never be equal [. . .]. The boy child has always been kind of more valued than a girl, from the society set up. . . . Of course, women will be bringing up their boys showing them that they are . . . super, even with more value than themselves, the mothers who gave birth to them. (Interviewee 19, Catholic nun)

Interviewee (49) has similar views to Interviewee (19), arguing that it is difficult to effectively achieve mindset changes in Kenyan traditional families, especially in the minds of farmers who believe that women are not permanent members of their nuclear family. Therefore, family heads will question the need to invest in the education of a female child who will become "a property" of another family as soon as they get married—they would think they are educating a girl child for somebody else (Interviewee 49, female, NGO's staff, and former government official). But seeing females as outsiders has an adverse outcome on all aspects of women's lives. For example, traditional families do not believe females add a meaningful value and therefore, they have no share in the family property, particularly in the distribution of land.

While customary practices in Kenya generally grant women secondary rights to land through their relationship to a male relative, they can rarely inherit the land on their own rights (Musangi 2017). Interviewee (30) attests that this is the case in his Luhya Tribe where a woman cannot claim the right to the land. "That is what we believe. I mean, that is a part of our culture!" (Interviewee 30, male, taxi driver). He proudly claims during our interview in Nairobi. Interviewee (31) makes a similar point as Interviewee (30) in relation to land rights, suggesting that female relatives should try their luck outside the family because, in his own words,

> Their rights are not the same as the men's [. . .] if they want to be married, they can be married. However, no access to family land, the land is for male siblings. . . . We say a female child will have to try her luck outside [the family]. (Interviewee 31, male, foreign-aid beneficiary)

On the other hand, Kenyan female education and well-being are compromised by parents' greed, not necessarily the culture, particularly in Maasai, Meru, Kisii, and other communities where arranged marriages of young girls to older men are made for the value of their dowries are common. Greedy parents or guardians would like to collect cows in dowries as soon as their female children hit puberty (Florence 2013, p. 378). My Interviewee (49) confirms Florence's points, suggesting that most families in remote Kenya believe that a girl should not go to school. As soon as she hits puberty, it is about time to move on because they want to collect cows for dowry (Interviewee 49, female, NGO's staff, and former government official). Speaking from lived experience, Interviewee (27) is emotional when she tells her story as a victim of parents' greed. She is living in hiding in Nairobi after she escaped from her father who wanted to marry her off before she even completed high school. He wanted the cows he would receive.

> Because I am a girl, he [my father] expected me to say, "Yes," and then I had to get married off. So, I refused, and he thought that I was just joking. So, the next day, he came with some people and so I thought they were our people because of the Christmas. . . . So, he [my father] called me and said, "This is the man you are going to . . . marry . . . and he has given me some cows." (Interview 27, female, high school student and foreign-aid beneficiary)

In terms of employment, Kenyan females have progressively fought their way into top leadership positions, including in politics, but their entry into male-dominated and patriarchal professions has led to a backlash. This is because the political inclusion of Kenyan females does not automatically lead to increased women's power broadly. There has not been a combination of bottom-up processes and top-down institutional efforts to transform gendered power relations (Berry, Bouka & Kamuru 2020, p. 1). My sample indicates that Kenyan families are against gender equity. Using a real-life example, Interviewee (6) explains how this works.

> I remember when we were implementing a project on women, peace, and security in a place called Bungoma. I talked to one of the ladies who was a champion of women's [rights], peace and security in her community. She told me, "I am trying to run for MCA (Member of County Assembly). I am trying to run a position, but . . . my own son is barring me from doing it." He says, "You know it's a man's job, it's not a women's job." (Interviewee 6, female, youth leader and civil society activist)

Gender-based violence has become a major human rights challenge for Kenyan women too. Odero et al. (2014, p. 784) say that gender oppression leads to sexual- and gender-based violence (SGBV), including intimate partner violence (IPV). John Gordon Simister (2010, p. 247) suggests that Kenyan patriarchal society prevents women from attaining power by means of domestic violence, particularly through financial, movement, and decision-making control. Auchter (2017, p. 1339) says that sexual- and gender-based violence can take different forms, including violent and painful circumcision of genitals in both men and women. Elizabeth Swart (2013, p. 40) makes a point that there is an association between gender-based violence, drug and alcohol abuse, sanitation, and the spread of sexually transmitted diseases (STDs), including HIV. Similarly, Njuki et al. (2012, p. 426) suggest that, while there are initiatives to help the victims of gender-based violence in Kenya, the lack of awareness and services, financial constraints of the victims, cultural beliefs, and stigma impede the overall success of intervention. As such, Simister (2010, p. 248) argues, the Kenyan society's lack of understanding of domestic violence and what it entails is of great concern. For example, Simister (2010, p. 248) further suggests 36 percent of Kenyan women do not think wife-beating is domestic violence. Evidence from my sample proves these authors correct. Interviewee (25) suggests that in Turkana, for example, the most common crimes are linked to the abuse against women and girls, including but not limited to sexual and physical assaults by male relatives, especially intimate partners (Interviewee 25, Male, foreign-aid beneficiary, and NGO's frontline staff). These points made by Interviewee (25) support Kim Thuy Seelinger's (2015, p. 546) findings that gang rapes are common in Kenya, particularly in times of global insecurity. They also support Ssewanyana et al.'s (2018, p. 189) suggestion that there is generally early sexual violence across generations in Kenya where 25 percent of the country's population experiences some form of sexual violence before they legally become adults. Interviewee (36), an expatriate who has worked in Kenya for several years, reports gross violations of human rights against women and men, but he is impressed by the Africans' resilience. He gives the example below:

> People have experienced despicable situations. People are raped, girls are raped, the[y have] HIV, but people are not losing hope. They are still determined to change their life, and to change the world, to change the environment. (Interviewee 36, Catholic priest, and NGO's executive)

Keller et al. (2017, p. 538) claim that recently, initiatives have been designed to improve Kenyan women's health and well-being by reducing the rates of gender-based violence, including prevention programs that motivate boys to change their attitude toward girls, intervene where necessary, and complement girls' empowerment programs. Evidence from my sample indicates that this is true, as Interviewee (8) attests. There used to be so much gender inequality because of the Kenyan socially constructed welfare systems where boys and men are given all opportunities. Nothing had changed until this slogan of *If you educate a woman, you'd educate the whole community* was promoted. So, this government-funded promotion of women's and girls' rights has had a great impact, changing the mindset of the citizenry at the grassroots level (Interviewee 8, female, university student). Interviewee (32) also sees some positive changes, arguing that females in his local community can now attain leadership positions. The issue of female circumcision has also been reduced in his village, despite UNICEF's (2020b) data indicating that 21 percent of Kenyan females aged between 15 and 49 had undergone the practice as per October 2020.

> In my tribe [. . .], nowadays, they [women] access their rights, but historically, as you know, they were circumcised. So, they did not have that freedom to decide themselves. But for now, in Kenya and, in fact, in my own county, the governor is a woman. (Interviewee 32, male, watchman)

The issue of gender inequality and sexual- and gender-based violence persists in Kenya, impeding the health and well-being of the most vulnerable populations and further undermining their human security.

Chapter 3

The Legacies of British Colonial Rule and Neo-Colonial Practices in Kenya

Central to this chapter are discussions involving a triangulation of the qualitative results with the literature from primary and secondary sources to demonstrate legacies of British colonial rule and neo-colonial practices for human security. The chapter points to the root causes of the current problems, and it particularly reveals Kenya's heavy-laden history that involved unabated draining of its wealth, including the historic land alienation. It also touches on the historic oppression of the indigenous Kenyans, including the torture and trauma that were inflicted upon indigenous Kenyans by colonial masters, the correlation between colonialism and gender inequality, the link between missionary work and gender inequality, and missionaries' manipulations and oppressive practices. This chapter finally touches on the notoriously evil "divide and rule" strategy, Kenya's dependence of external finance, the destruction of local systems and local markets, and the brain drain.

DRAINING AFRICA'S WEALTH AND LAND ALIENATION

African richness in terms of natural resources has historically been of limited benefit to indigenous Africans. Africa is the world's richest continent in terms of natural resources, and yet, it is home to the world's poorest people. African poverty also has its roots in the continent's first contact with Europeans, when they captured, enslaved, and sold African men and women for hard labor to the Americas, thus making huge profits at the expense of Africans (Anyangwe 2017). Even if some of the profits made from enslaved Africans were invested back into Africa, the profits made from these investments were quickly rechanneled to Europe, a move that further drained the continent's wealth (Mwaura 2005, p. 2). My participants held mixed feelings about what has gone wrong during the British colonial era in Kenya. The point made by Interviewee (56), who is a senior Australian government official of Caucasian background, for example, suggests that Anyangwe, Mwaura, and Hughes were correct. He argues that the removal of men and women in varying degrees of enslavement from key areas in Africa over centuries continues to affect African productivity today. As such, foreign-aid initiatives must deal with these complex situations because African resources and individuals who were fit to raise the continent to a higher level of performance were historically stolen, as he puts it:

> I think you could go back to Africans and their struggle. The massive slave trade that was taking large numbers of people out of Africa completely disrupted the economy, and you could draw comparable impacts to regional Australia when we took large numbers of the population, sent them to war and they did not come back. And multiple generations in regional towns have struggled. That is amplified on the African basis because, for centuries, we were taking men and women out of key areas. (Interviewee 56, male, Australian government official)

Interviewee (19) is a Kenyan nun who was a child during the colonial era, but she was old enough to remember what happened vividly. She shares the same views as Interviewee (56), as she suggests that colonial masters would come and take the strongest men from her village to go and fight in the First and Second World Wars. The removed men included Interviewee's (19) own great uncle. Her grandfather was only spared because he was young and too weak. Unsurprisingly, when they removed his brother from the family home, nobody questioned the oppressor, that is, the local colonial ruler (Interviewee 19, Catholic nun).

Besides, the exploitation of Kenyan natural resources and the construction of mining companies under the direct control of the British colonial government, Lotte Hughes (2008, p. 134) argues, is one of the many grievances Kenyan villagers hold, particularly people within the Maasai communities whose traditional land ownership was rendered void, losing their sole source of dignified livelihood. With a rapidly growing demand in the mining sector, the British colonial administration was willing to apply any tactics to acquire land in Kenya (Hughes 2008, p. 134). For example, a clause in the 1911 Maasai Agreement with the British government, which led to the local community's loss of a large portion of their land, was added by the then-governor after the Maasai representatives had put their thumbprints to the document as signatures (Hughes 2008, p. 134). This act of treachery paved the way for mining activities in the southern Maasai Reserve without informed consent or lawful agreement with the traditional owners of the land (Hughes 2008, p. 134).

It can be argued that actions by the former colonial masters still matter today because they delayed Kenyans' material progress and continue to shape Africans' daily life. Such trends need scholarly and policy attention for Africans to achieve meaningful changes psychologically, economically, and socially, particularly in relation to land and property rights (Waller 2012, p.5). This is particularly important in the Kenyan context, where the colonial administration created the so-called White Highlands concept and policy designed to ensure agricultural and fertile land was reserved for white settlers (Morgan 1963, p. 140). Evidence from my sample supports Morgan and Waller's findings. The legacies of colonialism imply that some Kenyan populations have suffered from intergenerational oppression and exploitation, as Interviewee (19), who clearly remembers the colonial practices throughout her childhood, attests:

> The white settlers, they came and took all the good [fertile] land. Good land. The best places. Go to Central and you find the White Highlands, especially . . . Of course, having been educated and what have you, they knew how to get the best places, the best parts, and they would plant like cash crops and now for us, as we grew up, we would go to pick coffee, their coffee, in [their] large plantations like from here, you can't see the end. (Interviewee 19, Catholic nun)

While the White Highland policy deprived African pastoral communities of essential resources for survival, it was justified by white settlers' and the international community's belief that Africans were not pastorally capable (Waller 2012, p. 5). Carey Jones (1965, p. 186) reveals that indigenous Kenyans did not regain access to the White Highlands until the 1960s when laws that had excluded African landownership from these areas were amended. Interviewee (10) gets visibly emotional while talking about the White Highlands. She briefly pauses and subsequently explains her emotions. These emotions center around the fact that some white settlers are still in Kenya and are still oppressing the locals even today.

> White highlands, honestly. How did someone come in a boat, owned land, and displaced whole communities? [. . .] You should go to Laikipia. People own large tracts of communal land . . . white men, up to now . . . 50 years after independence, yes. They still own large tracts of land and this is an area where it is predominantly the Masai—poor pastoralists who depend on land for their animals' survival. (Interviewee 10, female, academic and former official in the Kenyan department of foreign affairs)

The relationship between the colonial masters and the indigenous community was best defined as a continuous slave-master relationship (Behnam,

Azimi & Kanani 2017, p. 565), making locals powerless in their own country (Sheely 2016, p. 939). Therefore, as Evan Mwangi (2010, p. 87) would put it, when colonialists relinquished their powers, they essentially left a traumatized society open to elite manipulation, making it harder for community empowerment projects, including those funded through foreign aid, to achieve meaningful outcomes within the most vulnerable populations. That's why Kenya's land issues still shape politics, social cohesion, and the economy. Karuti Kanyinga (2009, p. 327) suggests that this situation has its roots in the process that saw the establishment of the British colonial administrators' economy. Behnam, Azimi and Kanani (2017, p. 565) argue that the land issue is particularly important in formerly colonized societies where, historically, a dominant group of individuals has made themselves superior and more deserving than others in society. Importantly, this colonial rhetoric places power firmly in the elites' hands, enhancing the existing intergenerational trauma that has historically shaped Kenyan society.

HISTORY OF TORTURE AND TRAUMA

Scholars such as Mwangi (2010, p. 87) argue that the brutalities suffered during the struggle for independence continue to affect Kenyans, particularly survivors, in different ways today. He suggests that survivors hugely celebrate independence while they also mourn the trauma caused by colonialism, displaying a mixture of delight and dismay. Similarly, Timothy H. Parsons (2017, p. 286) suggests that colonialists committed massacres in Kenya toward the end of the colonial era, particularly targeting the independence movement leaders, leaving them and their families dead or traumatized. Peter Leman (2011, p. 26) makes arguments along similar lines that many Kenyan national leaders, including Jomo Kenyatta who later became Kenya's first president following its independence in 1963, were tracked down, convicted, and sentenced to several years of hard labor for standing up for their rights. Mwangi (2010, p. 103) further argues that, while reliable archives and scholarly literature on the Kenyan colonial period are quite limited, there are growing emotional narratives highlighting the legacies of colonialism, its destructiveness, and the connection between the colonial government leadership style and the governance of Independent Kenya. Evidence from my sample does not deny the history of torture and trauma caused by major events during the colonial era. However, it suggests that Africans would like to move on, take responsibility, and refocus on the future of the continent as a strong and home to truly independent people, as Interviewee (29) explains:

> I am convinced that the coloniser caused us some problems. However, at some point, we should have been able to move on. You cannot convince me that from 1962 or 1961, we should keep complaining. As you can imagine, kids who were born 1962 are dying soon. They are old. If that person kept using this [colonialism] as an excuse, will even their children use the same excuse? That is the problem. (Interviewee 29, male, lieutenant general in the army)

But even the British government acknowledged in 2013 that some Kenyans were tortured during the Mau Mau Rebellion, and the court ruled that over 5,000 Kenyans who underwent torture could proceed with their compensation claims (BBC 2013). Despite this confession from the British side, my Interviewee (40) suggests that Kenyans and the rest of Africa should truly move on because blaming events that occurred more than fifty years ago for contemporary African hardships is wrong and distractive in nature. She argues that most African countries secured their independence in the 1960s, and it should not take so many years for countries to recover and rebuild (Interviewee 40, female, academic, and civil society activist).

Interviewee (56) suggests that the African case is unique and argues that other countries were colonized at the same time as Africa, but they have moved on and reached a sustainable level of performance locally, regionally, and globally. His argument aligns with Bhattacharya's (2019, p. 22) point that the colonists disrupted India's traditional trading patterns and shifted economic power to meet the needs and interests of the colonial rulers. Consequently, indigenous family firms progressively declined, and new methods of banking were introduced, destroying the traditional ways of doing business. However, by the twentieth century, local Indians had already changed these trends, rapidly expanding internal markets, particularly in the cotton industry. Interviewee (56) explains that if you look at a comparative country, India for example, the country was under colonial rule until roughly 50–60 years ago (77 years is the correct number as per 2024), which is roughly the same time as Kenya. Yet, they have been able to revolutionize and unite even though they have strong tribal and language differences. They have been able to create an economy, which is now a powerhouse in the world and hopefully they will overtake China in terms of GDP growth in the next 20 years. So, India has been able to thrive after the end of the colonial rule, unlike the African case (Interviewee 56, male, Australian government official).

At the end of the British colonial era in Kenya, Mwangi (2010, p. 103) further claims, the newly established African government reverted to the same colonial practices and progressively lost the ideals the Mau Mau Movement sought to achieve, creating an even wider gap between the rich and the poor. This left the disappointed Kikuyus, especially its young people, with no choice but to forge the Mungiki Movement under the same principles as the old Mau Mau; that is, fighting against injustice and oppression by the political elite (Kagwanja 2003, p. 25). These public disappointments mainly stem from a growing inequality gap (Mwangi 2010, p. 103). In fact, the Mungiki Movement was initially formed in the late 1980s as a religion-based on Kikuyu traditions. However, it quickly became a political movement that developed a notorious reputation for violence. Mungiki recruits its members from poor neighborhoods, namely from the poor and disenfranchised Kikuyu youth. Their slogans, such as "kazi kwa vijana" (Swahili for "jobs for the youth"), depict youth as marginalized from power and employment (Rasmussen 2010, p. 302). Such disparities will continue to shape Kenyans' daily lives and general human security, especially within the Kenyan female population, who are already vulnerable due to the forces of gender inequality, which, as the literature (Kassie, Ndiritu & Stage 2014, p. 153) suggests, have their roots in the colonial practices.

COLONIALISM, MISSIONARIES' WORK AND GENDER INEQUALITY

Although there has always been gender inequality in Kenyan society, this was heightened by white missionaries' practices and biblical teachings. For example, Anyangwe (2017) writes that colonialists came with missionaries who replaced African gods with Western religions and promoted restrictive Christian norms, which involved practices that plunged girls and women further into vulnerable positions. Therefore, Landon Schnabel (2016, p. 904) suggests, Christianity became a hindrance for progressive views and a reinforcing source of gender imbalance in all sectors of work, programs, and social life. Most of the participants who commented on the relationship between colonialism, missionaries, and gender inequality in Kenya today agree with Anyangwe and Schnabel, suggesting that these legacies make NGOs' work intended to close the gender gap much harder and complex in nature. Interviewee (34) is a female senior diplomat and a member of a conservative Christian church. She attests that missionaries used the Bible to enhance men's power in society, at the expense of women, when she claimed that missionaries used the Bible in order to say that the man was the head of the family, and they wanted to apply this in all sectors. That is why women felt like they should not even be going around outside their homes. So, women did not go further than the family property, making it impossible for them to participate in government-related work or other duties. That was exactly based on the word of God—be home and take care of children and husbands (Interviewee 34, female, diplomat). This point by Interviewee (34) explains Jude J. Ongong'a and Stephen I. Akaranga's (2014, p. 52) claim that when

European missionaries arrived in Kenya, their biblical teachings, including St. Paul's Letter to the Ephesians, 5:21–24, where women are reminded to submit to their husbands with reverence, demonstrated men's superiority and further undermined Kenyan women's social status. Interviewee (42), who is a senior Catholic priest, affirms that the colonial interpretation of the Bible played a great role in oppressing Kenyan women.

> I think many people have used [the] Bible to uphold and strengthen that gap. You know, that is very, very true. (Interviewee 42, Catholic priest, and academic)

On the other hand, Carolyn K. Lesorogol (2008, p. 554) writes that Western education was introduced in Kenya at the beginning of the twentieth century by missionaries, mainly to produce African male religious leaders to assist in the missionaries' work, giving no opportunity to women to access education whatsoever. Consequently, a very limited number of girls attended school until Kenya secured its independence in the 1960s, after which enrollments gradually increased. Interviewee (10) supports Lesorogol's points, adding that even other initiatives such as the airlift education scholarship scheme designed to educate Kenyans in Western countries to adequately prepare them for postcolonial Kenya did not include women. She makes a point that many of the females who were educated through the airlift scheme were coincidental as they initially accompanied their husbands to study abroad. Before that, only men were selected to pursue higher and quality education (Interviewee 10, female, academic and former official in the Kenyan department of foreign affairs). Besides, Ongong'a and Akaranga (2014, p. 51) argue that Kenyan traditions have always been shaped by oppressive socio-religious and cultural practices, which meant that women were socially and culturally looked down upon. They had no respectful social recognition but were despised, and Christianity as taught by the European missionaries enhanced this misogyny. Interviewee (22) agrees to some extent:

> Our Kenyan tribes are patriarchal, even before colonialism. It was an issue. For example, as a Luo, whether before colonial or post-colonial [era], a girl, for example, has no inheritance from the father's home. Did the colonial government bring that? And, it is unheard of that for example in Luo, a Luo woman would be a chief [. . .]. I really disagree with the fact that gender inequality emanates from colonialism and Christianity. It is our culture. (Interviewee 22, male, NGO's executive)

Most of these findings attest that Takatso Mofokeng (1988, p. 34) was right to claim that the missionaries' main interest in Africa was never to raise Africans to a higher level of performance, but to exploit them. That's why education was provided at a minimum level to give some indigenous members of the community skills necessary to function, but not high enough for them to become a threat. This is because missionaries and colonists were aware of the power of education—it was a key factor that led to excellent economic and technological outcomes during and after the British Industrial Revolution (Allen 2011, p. 357), and, in the African context, Western education was considered an important factor in Africans' prospects for self-determination (Sifuna 2006, p. 86). As such, some colonial administrations prevented their subjects from obtaining an optimal level of education as they feared this would lead to integration, enlightenment, and national identity, potentially equipping their slaves with the skills and tools necessary for revolt and struggle against the oppression they faced at the hands of colonists and missionaries (Friedman et al. 2016, p. 1).

MISSIONARY WORK AND OPPRESSION

Missionary work in Kenya involved some form of oppression. Roughly three decades ago, Mofokeng (1988, p. 34) demonstrated how the Bible was the vanguard tool carried to legitimate colonization and its practices of oppression and exploitation in Africa. Rebecca C. Hughes (2013, p. 825) establishes that this is true in the Kenyan context, where centralized missionary headquarters dictated the policies regarding the superiority of British culture and enforced the belief that only Western science, values, and practices could help raise African living standards. At the same time, Mofokeng (1988, p. 34) suggests, white missionaries were able to trick Africans to acquire their lands and a range of other resources, using the same superior status. This is neatly summarized by U.S. author, novelist, and activist James Baldwin (as cited in Bloom 2007) who claims that

> [. . .] when the white man came to Africa, the white man had the Bible and the African had the land, but now it is the white man who is being, reluctantly and bloodily separated from the land, and the African who is still attempting to digest or to vomit up the Bible [. . .]. (page 4)

As such, Bloom (2007, p. 4) claims, the white man's heaven was a black man's hell. Evidence from my sample stipulates that Mofokeng, Hughes, Baldwin, and Bloom were correct. Interviewee (42), a priest, suggests that religion was used by colonists and missionaries to manipulate and brainwash Kenyans. He argues that Africans were distracted by all these prayers. As they closed their eyes and thought about all these metaphysical realities, the white man was busy enriching himself and getting gold and materials. You can look at the place of religion in the West today as compared to Africa where religion is thriving, flourishing, mushrooming, with churches almost everywhere, but the social conditions are not following (Interviewee 42, Catholic priest, and academic). Interviewee (42) shares the same view as Interviewee (2) who, on top of concisely explaining Europeans' hypocrisy, argues that the indigenous community was tricked into strongly believing that worldly things did not matter, making it easier for the missionaries to steal their wealth, as he puts it:

> There is a big contradiction when one person is introducing Jesus to you, then the [his] brother is taking away your land, another brother is taking you as a slave, all of this. So, religion has been a very major weapon in brainwashing people. We are told, "Don't care about this world, we are going to heaven," and things like that. So, you follow that blindly and, before you know it, you don't have a country. (Interviewee 2, male, economist, and civil society activist)

Frederick Hale (2015, p. 54) makes a point that the European missionaries showed little respect to the locals whom they evangelized and sought to civilize. They viewed Africans as their inferior, naïve, childlike, empty, and God-forsaking, a move that encouraged the colonial system's attempt to destroy African culture and Africans' way of life. Dickson K. Nkonge (2014, p. 21) shares this view, adding that indigenous Kenyans had slim prospects for leadership or meaningful positions. They were judged as too inferior, unskilled, and uneducated to carry out expected tasks. Because of this superior attitude, Nkonge (2014, p. 21) suggests, it took four decades before the first black men were ordained in the church. According to my sample, Hale and Nkonge were correct. Interviewee (42) suggests that Africans were not considered humans. That's why all the indigenous systems and social organizations were rejected almost like nonexistent because "they were not people." That includes the traditional ways of relating to the environment, land, and customary laws, just to name a few. Colonialists and missionaries packed everything together—Africans' cultural practices, way of life, food, and religion—and threw them away. So, most of land in Kenya was state-owned to facilitate redistribution and use by missionaries (Interviewee 42, Catholic priest, and academic). Interviewee (10) further suggests that when the European missionaries arrived, they convinced Kenyans that all their traditional and religious structures and practices were wrong, and they had to be changed. Failing to do so would lead Africans to eternal life in hell, as she puts it:

> They told us that our religion is bogus . . . we were going to hell because we were witches . . . Their religion was the best. (Interviewee 10, female, academic and former official in the Kenyan department of foreign affairs)

The legacies of colonialism and missionaries' practices involving brainwashing and manipulation of the locals are still impacting on Kenyans' self-esteem today, as demonstrated by Interviewee (10) who made a point that if you go to any community and you put a white man and a black person together and just ask Africans, "Who do you think is smart between these two?" Of course, they would all suggest the white man is smarter (Interviewee 10, female, academic and former official in the Kenyan department of foreign affairs). Indeed, the findings and literature above demonstrate that a handful of white settlers and colonists easily gained control over the entire indigenous community. But how could a handful of white settlers gain control over the entire indigenous community in their own country? This question leads us to the issue of the divide-and-rule strategy made easier by the pre-colonial tribal divisions within Kenyan society.

DIVIDE-AND-RULE STRATEGY

Divide-and-rule strategy has enhanced tribal divisions and tensions in Kenya, but some of the current literature and accounts from my sample show that this is too simple to describe what the British administrators practiced. For example, Ray (2018, p. 367) does not entirely reject the idea that the ruling colonial strategists somehow disrupted the pre-colonial political and social trends, but describing their tactics as *divide-and-rule* is too easy and misleading as it renders the earlier historical tribal divisions irrelevant as we try to understand the current tensions (Ray 2018, p. 368). Similarly, Njororai (2009, p. 867) argues that Kenyan society has always been divided into ethnic groups, mostly with loose, fluid, and unstable formations. However, Njororai (2009, p. 867) claims, these ethnic identity differences were exacerbated by British colonial rulers in different ways, mainly through the colonial administrators' decision to reserve zones for only people with the same ethnic backgrounds. That's why settlement patterns based on ethnicity have persisted in Kenya despite recent political and economic developments that have increased social mobility among citizens (Njororai 2009, p. 867).

Evidence from my sample indicates that both Ray and Njororai were correct, as Interviewee (22), who voiced a great support for the colonial regime throughout our interview, attests. He argues that one of the very few things for which he would blame colonialists is the current issue of tribalism in Kenya. While tribes and divisions have always been there, he claims, the animosity among tribes has roots right from the colonial era, which spilled over into postcolonial regime. This is because the colonial regime stereotyped communities in Kenya, giving unfounded advantages to some communities at the expense of others (Interviewee 22, male, NGO's executive). Interviewee

(42) is of the same view and he explains how these divisions were practically achieved, arguing that, for example, Kikuyu people were systematically empowered and promoted at the expense of the rest of the tribes as a part of the divide-and-rule strategy.

> The Kikuyu have had that, like, you know, a step ahead of others, ah. Why Kikuyus? During colonial times, I think it was one of the strategies for colonialists to just identify one group and work with it—the divide and rule. So, the more you can extol one group, the better for the colonialists. (Interviewee 42, Catholic priest and academic)

Markham (2008) says that the colonial administration preferred the Kikuyu people mainly because they were more malleable than other historically aggressive tribes. The British settlers did not only employ them as laborers and servants, but they also gave them some education. Therefore, when Kenya secured independence, the Kikuyu people had a relative advantage as they had gained intellectual and educational abilities to run the country, giving them overwhelming power at the expense of many other tribal groups (Markham 2008). Accounts from my participants suggest that Markham was right about the privileges granted to the Kikuyu people during the colonial era, but they reject the assumption that the Kikuyu people are more malleable—they are not easy to manipulate. Rather, Interviewee (7) suggests, the Kikuyu people are sly—they know how to work with people, especially when they can see a clear endgame aligning with their interests. In other words, they can work with you to achieve their goals while people from Interviewee (7)'s tribe are too blunt, she claims. If they do not like something, they would make it clear because, culturally and historically, they never pretend they are fine when they are hurting inside. For the Kikuyu, they can hide their true feelings if they are going to get something meaningful at the end (Interviewee 7, female, NGO's executive).

Chege (2008, p. 127) writes that the first two decades of Kenyan independence were broadly characterized by success under the leadership of President Jomo Kenyatta. The market economy grew significantly, and this was a rarity among the economically failed states in Africa at the time. However, Chege (2008, p. 127) argues that toward the end of Kenyatta's rule, the regime was marked by rising intolerance, corruption, political assassinations, and widespread discontent over the dominance of Kikuyu in all aspects of Kenyan life. Similarly, Mark Huband (1992) argued that President Kenyatta failed to establish a balanced government, and that continued to haunt non-Kikuyu constituents for decades. Evidence from my sample suggests that Chege and Huband were correct. Interviewee (37) claims that the Kikuyu people are still the most privileged group in Kenyan society today. They dominate all companies, and those who have no contact or connections with them usually miss out on key aspects of Kenyan life, including employment and housing (Interviewee 37, female, university student).

The privileges enjoyed by the Kikuyu people at the expense of other tribes have historically triggered ethnic tensions and shaped Kenyan politics and society. For example, Marcel Rutten and Sam Owuor (2009, p. 306) claim that more than 1,100 Kenyans died in violence related to the general elections as recently as 2007. Additionally, over 350,000 were displaced because of unprecedented violence between the Luo and Kikuyu people who supported opposing political fronts. Saafo Roba Boye and Randi Kaarhus (2011, p. 100) suggest that recent ethnic clashes in Kenya are part of a century of hostility, a cycle of conflicts, and struggles over land and resources. They further suggest that the situation has gradually escalated as the citizenry has continued to congregate around tribal and ethnic groupings as the most effective way to ensure their own survival and access to core resources such as the land.

My participants' views align with Rutten and Owuor as well as Boye and Kaarhus's arguments. Today, the political government structure reflects the tribal divisions and therefore, activists such as Interviewee (40) refer to elected Kenyan officials as tribal chiefs. She makes a point that if an individual is from the Kikuyu Tribe, for example, they are majorly Kikuyu, 95 percent, and only 5 percent Kenyan. If they are from the Luhya Tribe, they are 95 percent a Luhya, only 5 percent whatever else. That's why even the voting intentions are influenced by one's tribe. As such, elected officials essentially become tribal chiefs rather than political leaders because this is a bunch of individuals from a certain community who get some goodies from the government and rechannel some of these back to their respective communities as a reward for the vote (Interviewee 40, female, academic, and civil society activist). The findings in this section mainly point to the adverse legacies of colonialism making it harder to achieve positive changes today, but it is equally important to objectively evaluate the possible good the colonial administration has done for Africa in general and Kenya in particular.

THE POSITIVE SIDE OF BRITISH COLONIAL RULE

The British colonial rule can be linked to some historical and major successes in former colonies, particularly in Kenya, as demonstrated by Ewout H. P. Frankema (2012, p. 335), who argues that the British influence has had positive outcomes on the performance of former colonies' institutions, capital investments, and postcolonial economic growth. Jonathan Lawley (2015, p. 267) makes a similar point, stating that the empire continued to share faiths, culture, fundamental values, and ties with its former colonies through the Commonwealth, based on the principles of equality. Frankema (2012, p. 335) adds that the British colonial rule's signature project was education, which became the most significant aspect of the British legacy not only in the Americas and Asia but also in Sub-Saharan Africa. This is evidenced through school enrollment data indicating that former British colonies register higher enrollments than the former French, Spanish, and Portuguese territories (Frankema 2012, p. 335).

Perhaps the bar was too low, but Interviewee (22) agrees that the British were better colonizers compared to the Belgians and Portuguese. As he puts it, the British put some solid infrastructures in place, and some of them are still being enjoyed by Kenyans today, including but not limited to universities and roads. On the other hand, some countries have had the Belgians who were completely exploiting as many resources as they could, as fast as possible, leaving nothing behind other than a completely traumatized society (Interviewee 22, male, NGO's executive).

British missionaries and the colonial administration agreed that the future of Africa relied on the moral, physical, and intellectual development of the African peoples, a position that was supported by European humanitarian organizations. According to them, education was not only necessary to achieve economic progress, but it could also help their mission to get the African people to an acceptable standard in terms of hygiene and other areas of concern (Matasci, Jerónimo & Dores 2020, p. 13). In the Kenyan context, the Kenyatta Administration's program for secondary schools was a continuation of a colonial education system, enhancing vocational training and development programs (Saeteurn 2017, p. 313). My Interviewee (50) agrees with this literature and suggests that Kenyans were able to learn from their colonizers, and hence improved their health, education, infrastructure, and other critical sectors, and she puts it:

> I can say that, through colonialism, . . . we as Kenyans, we are much, far much better compared [with] how it used to be because they brought [us] the issue of . . . education. Healthwise, we were able to improve our education, our health sector and infrastructure though it's not in all areas [. . .]. Through colonialism, we were able to adapt [learn] some[thing]. The best practices from them. (Interviewee 50, female, mental health program manager)

Mansour Gueye (2018, p. 118) argues that the colonial administration failed to transform African agriculture, claiming that Africans went into colonialism with a hoe and exited from it with the same. However, Saeteurn (2017, p. 313) argues that the underdevelopment of Kenyan agriculture is self-imposed as it mainly stems from the lack of interest in smallholder farming by ordinary Kenyans and the shortages in arable land. My evidence suggests that Saeteurn was correct here. There is a general lack of interest in agriculture, particularly with young Kenyan populations, as Interviewee (39), a policymaker and senior government official, argues. If Kenya really wants to improve socially and economically, he postulates, they must make agriculture the backbone of their economy. More importantly, he further argues, the Kenyan government must make agriculture attractive to young people. Currently, it is very difficult to convince a young Kenyan to be involved in farming. Many young people leave their ancestral land for the city centers, even if that means a life with uncertainty (Interviewee 39, male, Kenyan government official).

Evanson N. Wamagatta (2009, p. 371) praises the strategic importance of British East Africa's infrastructure projects, including several railway lines completed toward the nineteenth century. They opened the interior of Kenya and attracted foreign presence and investments but to the intensification of colonialism. For these projects were motived by the Europeans' desire for African dominance, in Kenya's case, British dominance. Despite this, Charis Enns and Brock Bersaglio (2020, p. 102) argue that such projects still benefited the locals as these colonial infrastructures connected inaccessible areas to key administrative centers and ports. My sample agrees, with Interviewee (39) suggesting that the colonial administration did its best to put in infrastructures, but in whose interests?

> These people [colonialists] did their best. If it is in terms of infrastructure, they managed even to build railways for us [. . .]. They came, they put infrastructures, but they never went with them in [back to] Europe [meaning these infrastructures remained in Kenya to benefit Kenyans]. (Interviewee 39, male, Kenyan government official)

More surprisingly, Interviewee (22) argues that the colonial regime achieved more than the African indigenous leaders, even if he is still ambivalent about the British presence in Africa, claiming that looking at what they put in place and what the African leaders have done, the British colonial rulers went too early, but also comparing to other places where they stayed too long, it was the right time that they went (Interviewee 22, male, NGO's executive). Currently, many of the colonial infrastructures are being replaced, modernized, or expanded by external actors. These developments have recently sparked a debate on whether the latest infrastructural privatization scramble in the region has emancipatory potential (Enns & Bersaglio 2020, p. 102). The benefits of neo-liberal privatization, per neo-liberal assumptions, are that these will trickle down to everyone (Monbiot 2016). The literature and findings that follow will test this idea looking at whether Kenya is still at risk of imperialism vis-à-vis neo-liberal practices.

THE ROLE OF NEO-COLONIALISM AND IMPERIALIST PRACTICES

Kenya and East Africa have always been the testing grounds for neo-colonialism. Even if all East African countries theoretically secured independence decades ago, their economic and political policies are usually dictated by foreign powers (Maekawa 2015, p. 317). William I. Robinson (2011, p. 349) suggests that developing nations' social structures have significantly changed in recent decades due to the forces of globalization. These nations have, Robinson argues, willingly or unwillingly become incorporated into global markets, meaning that emerging, transnationally oriented elites compete with former nationally oriented elites who are more protected and stronger, and this implies that the weaker in the chain will lose. Evidence from my sample suggests that Maekawa and Robinson were correct, with Interviewee (34) arguing that African countries have only gained their independence in theory because most of the critical decisions they make are dictated by foreign powers (Interviewee 34, female, diplomat). Similarly, Jerry Harris (2014, p. 313) makes a point that even if the capitalist expansion has created a transnational economic system, many national forms and expressions of capital remain the weaker link in the chain. Consequently, rivalries and reciprocal influences between states are still expressed (Harris 2014, p. 313). This literature aligns with Interviewee's (42) points, but he goes a bit further to suggest that resisting the Western actors' pressure means political suicide for African leaders, as was the case for President Robert Mugabe of Zimbabwe. He explains:

> So how much clout do African governments have when you have every incentive to follow what the big brothers are dictating because . . . you've seen what happened to [President Robert] Mugabe when he said, "No," to some of the Western policies. To say, "No" to those who have more power and more capabilities than you, it can be a political suicide that you are committing, and you have to negotiate. (Interviewee 42, Catholic priest and academic)

More alarmingly, Obeng-Odoom (2015, p. 246) suggests that even the notion that Africa is on the rise and ripe for foreign investments is a myth. It involves processes that enable the powerful in the world order to plunder African common goods. Interviewee (9) holds similar views, arguing that even with the forces of globalization, East Africa does not benefit meaningfully because the region does not have what it takes to become a strategic player. This is because, he claims, in terms of technology, for example, Africans are not able to meaningfully compete with actors from advanced economies because their technology is too old and weak. Logically, meaningful competitions cannot occur until Africans are able to use the same speed, which will take a very long time (Interviewee 9, male, colonel in the army). On the other hand, the world order is shaped by strategic relationships, with Africa so poorly connected that it remains impossible for the continent to safeguard its interests at global scale. More alarmingly, Kenyans feel like even the UN and its agencies are not designed to protect the interests of the weaker Africans in the chain, as Interviewee (2) argues:

> When you have something called the UN—United Nations. The United Nations is a system that is aimed [designed to] profit the countries that are in the Security Council. . . . Then, you have other agencies, the UN agencies, that are spread all over through UNDP [United Nations Development Program], UNEP [United Nations Environment Programme], UN Habitat [United Nations Human Settlements Programme], then you have [the] World Bank. So, anything that is monetary, development [or] currency, they make sure that whatever was set as imperialism is maintained. . . . I keep saying, "Kenya if you want to be respected, come out of the UN." And it is like no one thinks that is possible. People are scared. (Interviewee 2, male, economist, and civil society activist)

Briefly, Africa has historically failed to secure genuine autonomy and an influential place in the world order. Here, I submit that any success in changing the status quo will depend on the continent's progress in finding durable solutions to its resource robbery by rich nations and securing financial autonomy.

KENYA'S DEPENDENCE ON EXTERNAL FINANCE

Accounts from my Kenyan sample affirm the literature indicating that the African continent's overreliance on external funding to sustain itself financially renders its political independence void. Maekawa (2015, p. 317) writes that neo-colonialism quickly gained ground in newly independent countries in Africa due to their immediate inability to secure political and economic independence simultaneously. This led to further dependence on foreign aid, embedding favorable conditions for the survival of the colonial systems and structures (Maekawa 2015, p. 317). Most of my participants agree with Maekawa, suggesting that the colonial structures and systems remain intact in Africa today mainly due to the continent's chronic dependence on the international community to fund its domestic programs. For example, my Interviewee (40) submits, colonialism has never truly left Africa. This is because, in theory, the colonial masters gave African indigenous leaders an independence shaped by nominal power; that is, they found other, more effective and covert ways to continue colonizing the people of Africa through foreign aid (Interviewee 40, female, academic, and civil society activist). As such, as Julia Vorhölter (2012, p. 284) rightfully puts it, the Western world continues to dictate the African way of life today, constantly interfering in their internal affairs, particularly in the areas of politics, governance, gender, kinship, and sexuality. Similarly, Chibuike Uche (2015, p. 355) suggests that developed nations exert control over poor countries through economic penetration, political subversion, and military pressure, and my Interviewee (39), a senior Kenyan government official familiar with Kenya's international relations, attests:

> Still, I can tell you that the West . . . really has a lot of say in how we do our things, in most developing countries, and I have told you the reason behind it, that these people fund our economy either by loans that they give us, eh, by the investments that they bring in our country, you know [. . .]. We actually tend to bend some of the things that we are doing to fit their requirements. (Interviewee 39, male, Kenyan government official)

Langan (2015, p. 103) makes a similar point that developed countries offer budget support to poor countries, but with several conditions, some of which undermine their own sovereignty and values. Using what's happening in Kenya as an example, Interviewee (55) endorses this literature when she says that Kenya's counter-terrorism agenda is driven by Americans, for example. So, whatever America says, Kenyan policymakers just take it all in (Interviewee 55, female, lawyer). The point made by Interviewee (55) explains my Interviewee's (29) frustrations when he complains about cashed-up foreign actors using their financial superiority to drive their agenda in Africa—"They can interfere using human rights [project] as an excuse—women emancipation, homosexuality, freedoms [. . .]. When they notice you do not protect their interests, they will stop all aid, they cut everything and start implementing sanctions" (Interviewee 29, male, lieutenant general in the army). These findings and literature demonstrate that financial dependence undermines Kenyan independence, adversely affecting Kenyans' ability to sustain their local markets and become significant competitors in the global markets and supply chains.

THE STRATEGIC DESTRUCTION OF THE LOCAL SYSTEMS AND LOCAL MARKETS

Some international actors strategically destroy African local markets and systems for their own self-survival reasons. As such, even if some foreign-aid-funded projects are designed to improve local production, it does not lead to financial improvement because there is no good market for African products. Therefore, African actors simply give up. Walden Bello (2008, p. 453) writes that decades ago, African countries were net food exporters, but this trend had reversed by the end of the colonial era. Almost every African nation has become a net importer throughout recent years, with the continent importing about 25 percent of its food. Due to globalized capitalist industrial agriculture, Bello (2008, p. 453) further suggests, emerging countries have progressively been integrated into a system where export-oriented production is dominated by large industrial farms, leaving limited room for poor financial performers. Besides, Singer (1989, p. 198) makes a point that African food prices are relatively low in the international market because of food aid, reducing the motivation to increase domestic production, and my Interviewee (28) agrees. He gives an example from his lived experience:

> Let me talk about tea, which my family has. It is just a small farm. There is a factory that processes that tea, and it is put into the market, but I don't know how they do it. And Kenyan tea is the best, I have heard [. . .]. You are from Australia, right? I think you can get Kenyan tea there. But [the] marketing strategy isn't . . . good enough. [. . .] Many farmers are cutting down the tea because it does not have a good return . . . the lack of market, that is what I think. (Interviewee 28, male, NGO's frontline staff)

The statement above supports Soini's (2005, p. 157) submission that Tanzanian farmers' life standard does not improve due to poor prices allocated to their coffee in the world market. This point is also shared by V. Muisyo and M. Ibrahim (2018) who argue that poor prices, coupled with the flooding of local markets, systematically destroy vital African industries. My sample have similar views to those of Bello, Singer, and Soini as well as Muisyo and Ibrahim. For example, my Interviewee (32) suggests that the lack of global and African markets has rendered farming in Kenya unattractive as the activity is no longer financially worth the effort. He explains that they grow good things, including coffee, maize, and beans, but they have nowhere to sell them at a reasonable price, and that is true in Kenya and other parts of Sub-Saharan Africa (Interviewee 32, male, watchman).

Africans' inability to become competitive on a global scale has roots in the destruction of the indigenous local markets, social, political, and economic systems by external actors, as demonstrated by Tanni Deb and Chris Giles (2018), who explain that the fishing trade had become the mainstay for communities alongside Lake Victoria, securing employment for locals for decades until recently when cheap Chinese fish imports came into Kenya, destroying the existing industry. In 2016 alone, China exported around $30 million of fish to Kenya (Deb & Giles 2018). Deb and Giles's claims are confirmed by my participants, with Interviewee (1) suggesting that the Chinese fish is even cheaper.

> There is a lot of infiltration of foreign fish, including Chinese fish, which, apparently seems to be cheaper than the fish from Lake Victoria. If you happen to go to the western part of the country, fish there is more expensive than the fish you find in Nairobi. (Interviewee 1, male, civil society activist and economist)

But the destruction of local African markets targets more sectors than just the agriculture and fishing industries. Emily Anne Wolff (2020, p. 2) suggests that, as recently as 2018, the United States engaged in a trade war with the East African Community's member states, including Kenya, Uganda, and, particularly, Rwanda after the latter strongly advocated for the phasing out of the importation of second-hand clothes. As Sinha et al. (2012) suggest, the disadvantages associated with second-hand clothes imports to Kenya and Tanzania outweigh the claimed benefits—they destroy the local textile industry, as Interviewee (42) said:

> I don't know if you followed the case of "mitumba" [Swahili term for "second-hand clothes"], the second-hand clothes, which was discussed and debated at the East African community. The East African Community wanted to stop importing the second-hand clothes and said, "We need to develop our textile industry." The lobby in the US managed, all the way to the White House . . . and the White House had to force African governments to say, "You can't adopt that policy. You have to relax it because we have this deal, partnership." Kenya and Tanzania backed off. (Interviewee 42, priest, and civil society activist)

Unfortunately for the African economy, a range of conditions are imposed on African actors in a way that they remain with no other viable options than selling their products in a raw state, which limits the benefits generated from these. Interviewee (7) affirms this phenomenon, claiming that Africans are forced to sell raw materials because they do not have manufacturing capabilities. There is also constant manipulation by Western countries, which apply stereotypes against African actors and African products as inferior and never good enough. Kenya and other African countries export coffee and tea, for example. However, they are always told their tea is not good enough and, therefore, they must mix it with Pakistani tea for it to be better (Interviewee 7, female, NGO's executive). Based on the findings in this section, it is evident that Kenya requires highly educated public servants to design and drive policies to strengthen its local market and improve its competitiveness globally. Unfortunately, as Alberts (2007, p. 142) puts it, brain drain practices have meant that highly trained Africans in the West rarely go back to Africa upon the completion of their study programs.

BRAIN DRAIN

I do not dispute that Africans who complete their study programs in the West rarely return home and use their acquired skills to develop their mother continent, but based on accounts from my sample, I reject the idea that African students are targeted and manipulated by the West to remain there. Mohamed A. El-Khawas (2005, p. 40) suggests that given the low quality of education at the domestic level, some African students are sent to countries such as France, the United Kingdom, the United States, and Germany to pursue their education at the best universities possible, and they are expected to come back home and contribute to nation-building, but only a handful of them return upon completion of their programs. My Interviewee (2), who holds a PhD in Economics, disagrees and makes a point that there is no shortage of highly educated individuals in Africa, as he puts it:

> We have all these people with PhDs or whatever skills, inside Africa. [They are] not going anywhere, but they are not doing anything. We suffer [. . .]. For him, he is hurt more from brain haemorrhage than brain drain. Because [let] say the numbers . . . ok people leave, but what are the numbers compared [to] those who remain? (Interviewee 2, male, economist, and civil society activist)

But Alberts (2007, p. 141) claims that brain drain is a reality. He gives the example of African students who go to the United States, apply for a work visa upon completion of their study, and eventually adjust their residence status to become "permanent residents." The initial "temporary" migrant status, Alberts (2007, p. 142) argues, becomes "highly skilled permanent resident," to the benefit of the United States and at the expense of their home country. Hailay Gebretinsae Beyene (2015, p. 145) also affirms that Kenya, Ethiopia, and Nigeria fare best as to this documented African diaspora across the world. Evidence from my sample indicates that El-Khawas, Alberts, and Beyene are correct in relation to the failure of African students to return home upon completion of their study programs. However, my sample indicates, the real reason most African students do not return to Africa is the general lack of opportunities in the continent, not brain drain, as Interviewee (22), addressing the researcher directly, explains:

> [John] Bosco, put yourself here. You have your daughter; at home you don't give your daughter a chapati [Swahili word for "pancake"]. The daughter go[es] to the neighbour, there is chapati. The following day, the daughter goes to [get the] chapati. You know, you might end up losing your daughter to the neighbour because of just a chapati. So, when Kenyans go to Europe or to the [United] States, they find better remuneration packages, and better living standards of course. (Interviewee 22, male, NGO's executive)

Interviewee (42) makes a similar point in relation to the lack of opportunities in Africa, but he goes a bit further and argues that great talents in Africa are threatened by insecure and ambitious elites. He claims that African elites usually love fighting against and destroying geniuses. They do not like people who shine. And the moment you become a threat to their ambitions, they will do everything possible to block you, even if it requires eliminating you physically (Interviewee 42, priest and academic).

By 1987, the number of highly educated Africans leaving the continent annually peaked at 80,000, most of whom migrated to their former colonial power (El-Khawas 2005, p. 37). Besides, when African students decide to leave their host countries at the completion of their study programs, they do not always go back to their home countries (Hurst 2017, p. 51). The analysis of migration patterns of overseas students from Kenya, Zambia, Malawi, Nigeria, Ghana, Democratic Republic of the Congo, Uganda, and Zimbabwe demonstrated that many Africans who had studied in the United Kingdom, the United States, and European countries went to South Africa upon graduation, where they accepted academic positions (Hurst 2017, p. 51). This literature suggests that there is also internal brain drain from the African continent to South Africa, with countries such as Kenya as victims. Whatever the reason might be, the issue of brain drain remains complex in nature and, through the findings in this section, it is evident that, without meaningful employment and uncorrupted promotional opportunities in the continent, mass migration patterns of highly skilled professionals out of Africa will continue to leave most countries with shortages in skills they need to partake in the twenty-first-century competitive world (El-Khawas 2005, p. 37), making it impossible for them to wean themselves off foreign aid.

Chapter 4

History and Processes of Foreign Aid

Even if the number of foreign-aid donors to poor and middle-income countries has progressively increased over the years, this chapter mainly examines the negatives of the foreign-aid history and processes. Traditionally, the Development Assistance Committee, a body established by the Organisation for Economic Cooperation and Development (OECD) member states, acted as a forum to discuss poverty reduction and aid development. The committee progressively became a core component of the global development architecture (Mawdsley 2010, p. 361). It consists of 24 members, including 23 industrialized nations and the European Commission. The International Monetary Fund (IMF), the World Bank, and the United Nations Development Program (UNDP) have the status of observer. Over two decades ago, Emma Mawdsley (2010, p. 361) claims, other countries, including but not limited to Brazil, China, Hungary, Iceland, India, Poland, and Saudi Arabia, started giving a significant portion of aid on an annual basis. The international aid community generally targets education and youth employment, with the main agenda of enhancing policies and programs designed to expand youth entrepreneurship and civil society (King 2018, p. 135).

The Official Development Assistance (ODA), also administered by the Organisation for Economic Cooperation and Development (OECD 2020), consists of grants and concessional loans. Grants do not come with any repayment obligations as they are a pure transfer of cash from the donor government to the receiving country. In contrast, the concessional loans principal amount must be repaid with accrued interests. However, they are extended on favorable terms that amount to a grant equivalent of at least 25 percent; that is, the difference between the principal and the discounted value at the time of the repayment obligation (Brech & Potrafke 2014, p. 63). Funds are either distributed as bilateral aid directly from government-to-government or through a multilateral organization (Quazi et al. 2019, p. 284).

African countries also receive military aid. The United States and the European Union are the leading donors based on their shared interests to fight against terrorism (Jowell 2017, p. 110). Such aid helps Kenya and the region to establish peacekeeping training centers as a part of the broader military assistance programs provided by bilateral or multilateral donors. The aid is intended to boost African troops' professionalism, knowledge about international norms, and provide a space for socialization, forging bonds, and ties for better security outcomes in the continent (Jowell 2017, p. 102). On the other hand, even if the international community sometimes fails to raise enough funds to meet the needs identified by the UN, they usually raise billions of dollars annually directed to help people affected by humanitarian crises across the world as a part of international humanitarian assistance (Puri et al. 2017, p. 519) and a range of projects target Kenya (Nikulkov et al. 2016). The United States is also heavily engaged in programs to support good governance in Kenya (Foreign Aid Assistance 2017). These programs are intended to create good conditions for community empowerment and to ensure Kenyans enjoy basic human rights as determined by international humanitarian law (De Zayas 2014, p. 259). Similarly, knowing that around 45 percent of global under-five children's deaths are caused by undernutrition, the international community has established the international food assistance scheme. In 2016, the United States increased its cash-based food assistance, and Kenya was one of the main beneficiaries (Nikulkov et al. 2016).

On top of a rapidly growing education and training cooperation with Kenya, China invests heavily in Kenya's infrastructure through its direct foreign investment (King 2010, p. 488). Such developments are not coincidental. As Jerry Harris (2018, p. 1716) puts it, China is renowned for its historic allegiance to Third World solidarity. In fact, Harris argues, there is no greater commitment to African or Asian governments with a socialist orientation than that offered by China. Similarly, Jodie Yuzhou Sun (2019, p. 42) suggests that the relationship between China and Africa is one of the longest, dating from the dawn of African states' independence. For instance, following the 1955 Bandung Conference, China strengthened its diplomatic relations with African and Asian countries, subsequently creating West Asian and African Affairs Departments in China's Foreign Ministry.

In the 10-year period prior to Australian Prime Minister Tony Abbott's election victory in 2013, Australian foreign-aid spending increased by 80 percent in real terms. Soon after the Liberal National Party (LNP) took power, the Abbott government made significant aid policy changes, cutting the aid budget three times in a period of 15 months (Day 2016, p. 641). The newly elected government also integrated the Australian Aid Agency (AusAID) into its Department of Foreign Affairs and Trade. Within months of the LNP election victory, AusAID no longer existed, and the scope and structures of Australian aid programs were changed at a considerable speed (Day 2016, p. 641). Australia's foreign aid to the whole Sub-Saharan Africa was around A$136 million in Official Development Assistance in the 2016–17 financial year, a 65 percent decrease in foreign aid to the same region from the 2012–13 financial year where A$385 million was spent (DFAT 2014).

The post-independence era saw a boom in NGOs and civil society groups in Kenya. The sector has progressively evolved over decades, starting with missionary groups such as the Christian Council of Kenya (CCK), which was later known as the National Council of Churches in Kenya (NCCK), and the African Medical and Research Foundation (AMREF) (Kimemia 2013, p. 21). By the end of 1980, Kenya counted more than 500 national and international organizations, an increase of 272 NGOs from 1970 (Kimemia 2013, p. 23). In the period between 1997 and 2006, the number of NGOs in Kenya had increased by over 400 percent (Matthews 2017). By 2014, the country was home to 9,728 registered NGOs, 7,258 of which were active. In the 2013–14 financial year alone, 1,800 NGOs were set up in Kenya (Karanja & Kilonzo 2015). Even with some proven positive results, the u*ncertainty around the* role of foreign aid in reducing poverty has, historically, triggered controversial debates (Snowdon 2009, p. 247).

FOREIGN AID CONTROVERSIES

Foreign aid to Sub-Saharan African countries, including Kenya, is controversial. Dambisa Moyo (2017) argues that foreign aid plunges Africa into perpetual poverty and dependence, while William Easterly (2003, p.25) suggests that foreign aid never reaches the poor who deserve it most due to corrupt practices. Therefore, Brian Snowdon (2009, p. 247) concludes, any suggestion of its increase to Sub-Saharan Africa usually faces significant backlash because the debates around foreign aid have always been plagued with issues of causality, measurement, feasibility, politics, and ideologies. In contrast, Jeffrey Sachs (2014) and Adeniyi J. Adedokun (2017, p. 184) are optimists and suggest that foreign aid is an important tool to alleviate poverty and promote growth.

Evidence from my sample does not entirely reject Easterly's suggestion that foreign aid can be captured in bad governance and corrupt practices. Nor does it contrast Snowdon's points in relation to issues of foreign-aid measurement and feasibility. However, it aligns more with Sachs's and Adedokun's views. Here, my evidence suggests that some form of foreign aid reaches and significantly improves the living conditions of the most vulnerable members of Kenyan society, some of whom entirely depend on it to survive. Most of my evidence also rejects Moyo's suggestion that foreign aid to Africa does not make any difference. Such a position is not only misleading, but it is also dangerous. Interviewee (40) is a global studies program director at one of the universities in Nairobi with direct knowledge and experience of foreign-aid-funded programs. She and several other participants suggest that foreign aid has been instrumental in improving the health and well-being of vulnerable Kenyans. For example, Interviewee (40) explains, foreign-aid-funded programs have had a significant impact on the reduction of HIV infections. She makes a point that Kenya has benefited from the Global Fund on HIV, which, at some point, faced challenges in terms of corruption, but it still helped in terms of fighting against HIV/AIDS through campaigns—"seek medication and get ARVs" (Interviewee 40, female, academic and civil society activist). Foreign aid has also complemented the Kenyan government's work, especially during natural disasters and other emergencies, Interviewee (40) further claimed during our many discussions. Her points were supported by Interviewee (25), who suggested that the impact of the complementary role of foreign aid is obvious within Kenyan society, as he puts it:

> Foreign aid is good. This is because there are some initiatives the government would like to implement, but sometimes they do not have enough [money] to fund their budget. That [foreign aid] money becomes complementary. Even if we claim that the money reaching an average citizen is insignificant, we can clearly see a range of projects being initiated, with some of the work being done. (Interviewee 25, male, foreign-aid beneficiary, and NGO's frontline staff)

In contrast, P. T. Bauer (1974, p. 169) suggested five decades ago that foreign aid was not necessary or enough to generate material progress. Therefore, Bauer did not see the urgency or the need for the international community's intervention because he did not believe people in developing countries were genuinely poor. Such conclusions could stem from the lack of disaggregated data on the impacts of foreign aid on the receiving population, an indication that the quality and benefits of this scheme remain unmeasured (Easterly & Williamson 2011, p. 1930). What has been proven, however, is that despite the estimated transfer of more than $4.6 trillion in Official Development Assistance (ODA) to developing countries since the 1960s, most part of the world's population still live under conditions of extreme poverty (Easterly & Williamson 2011, p. 1930). Interviewee (1) makes a point that contradicts both Bauer as well as Easterly and Williamson, claiming that foreign aid has been instrumental in bringing about positive changes within Kenyan society through education, community empowerment, and mindset change initiatives, particularly in rural and remote regions—a great start.

> Foreign aid has actually also opened up development in very remote areas because, through one developing [development] initiative like a health facility or a school, then people begin to see things differently. It contributes towards behaviour attitude and mindset change, which is part of what we do. [. . .] [For] some of the communities we work with, the guns used to be their working sticks. They were not willing to be disarmed. They have currently accepted. They have given back their arms and this has basically reduced the number of deaths. (Interviewee 1, male, economist, and civil society activist)

There is no denial that the level of corruption has historically had a negative impact on the effectiveness of foreign aid and other developments in Kenya, as demonstrated by John Harrington and Ambreena Manji (2013, p. 4) who say that bribery and other corruptive behaviors are features of Kenyan daily life. Corruption is experienced from the interactions between average citizens, police, and public servants to elaborate networks linking the state and commercial sectors. Similarly, Michael Wrong (2014) says that Kenyan citizens must reach into their pockets to get anything done simply because most of the people in society are corrupt, and giving bribes in return for public services is a norm. Evidence from my sample indicates that the literature above is correct. Interviewee (21) is an expatriate from Spain who had been working in an international organization in Kenya for two years at the time of the interview. She also claims that corruptive practices affect everyone and every sector in Kenya, and that corruption has reached a level where anyone could bribe a police officer, in a police uniform, with 50 Kenyan shillings [approximately USD0.50], openly (Interviewee 21, female, expatriate).

Besides, there are large-scale corruption scandals involving senior government officials. As such, corruption impedes the effectiveness of new and old initiatives, including in the critical area of public health (Friedman 2018, p. 13). For example, antiretroviral drugs (ARVs), which HIV-infected people depend on for survival, are available in Sub-Saharan Africa. But unfortunately, corruption has become the main barrier for ARVs to get to those who need them and prevent AIDS deaths. Clinics distribute ARVs disproportionately and unfairly to areas where residents are predominantly of the same ethnicity as the incumbent political leader (Friedman 2018, p. 13). Besides, Kenyan officials who occupy high-level positions usually stay in power for life. They distribute the public-sector positions and resources to their associates and family, making no distinction between state-owned and private business (Hibbard 2015, p. 2). My sample totally agrees, with Interviewee (11) suggesting that those who steal public funds usually target big sums of money.

> If we look at our news, the billions and billions [are] being stolen and . . . that money is not [never] recovered, and more and more is still being stolen [. . .]. They are Kenyans who steal from Kenyans . . . because like these big, big

> companies, if you have a post [position] somewhere, it is like they say, "Don't steal little money, you steal good money so that even if you are convicted, you've done something." (Interviewee 11, female, NGO's frontline staff)

The misuse of foreign-aid funds has left some donors with no option but to adopt restrictive measures (Harrington & Manji 2013, p. 4). For example, the United Kingdom suspended all its financial aid for free primary school education in Kenya in 2010 after it was revealed that £880,000 out of a £20 million budget had been diverted from its intended purpose (Harrington & Manji 2013, p. 4). And this was just one of the many examples of corruption scandals in Kenya, some of which cost the country hundreds of millions of dollars (Harrington & Manji 2013, p. 4).

There is also this famous concept of "[. . .] our turn to eat," implying that Kenyan leaders worry more about their personal or own ethnic group's financial benefits than the public good (D'Arcy & Cornell 2016). Moreover, donor governments and agencies generally do not have enough information about the most deserving population in the receiving country. They often delegate the responsibility to corrupt government officials to consider the allocation and distribution of foreign-aid funding. Senior officials take advantage of this discretion to allocate foreign-aid funds in a way that further enhances their political and personal status at the expense of the deserving, poor Kenyans (Jablonski 2014, p. 294). Evidence from my sample confirms that the diversion of public funds from their intended purpose is a reality in Kenya. Interviewee (20) is an economist who closely monitors the Kenyan government's financial dealings. He puts it this way:

> The Kenyan budget runs to trillions of shillings [and] almost half [of it] is donor-funded, either from other governments or other agencies, but how much is spent on what it is required is the question. (Interviewee 20, male, NGO's executive)

Meredith DeBoom (2019, p. 16) suggests that sovereign debt creates a unidirectional relation of power in which the lender holds all the cards. For example, it is suggested that the infrastructure loans from the Chinese government to Africa are designed to keep Africans in perpetual debt in the so-called Chinese debt-trap diplomacy (DeBoom 2019, p. 16). Wang Yiwei (2018) questions if the attention on the Chinese debt trap by Western critics necessarily means the West really cares about poor countries' vulnerability to the Chinese loan practices or they are simply concerned about their compromised position as they compete for interests in the region and China's progressive attempt to become a dominant global player. Deborah Brautigam and Meg Rithmire (2021) are less diplomatic and call the fear of the Chinese "dept trap" a myth. On the other hand, scholars such as Jean-Claude Berthélemy (2006, p. 179) argue that these reactions have two sides, and Africa is simply a battlefield. Berthélemy suggests that the motives of foreign-aid givers comprise egoistic behavior where donors link aid to their self-interests, and altruistic behavior where they try to meet recipient needs. Evidence from my sample suggests that international actors in Africa are there for their own self-survival interests first and foremost, and Africa simply remains a battlefield. Interviewee (39) explains:

> When somebody like control[s] your economy, he has a big say on what is happening in your country, and when he gives you money to do something, then he has an interest, of course, so that he can also benefit in one way or the other or wants things done in certain a way. And we can see when a lot of funds come from China, then we tend to go the China way [inaudible]. The same thing when the UK government, the Europeans, the USAID actually in some particular fields, then things happen in the way they want. (Interviewee 39, male, Kenyan government official)

Even NGOs can have two paradoxical sides, Anil Rajput (2019) suggests. Apart from their obvious humanitarian work, their other role could be as a tool for foreign powers to channel their propaganda, serving as proxies for foreign entities and destabilizing the progress and stability of the host nation. Interviewee (56), a senior Australian government official who has previously worked in the Department of Foreign Affairs and Trade, does not believe the foreign-aid policy agenda is necessarily designed to destabilize the receiving country. However, he agrees that the donor country's national interests come first.

> My understanding is [that] you got to look at aid for every country through lenses of national security first. So, what's the national interest that you are trying to advance through aid schemes? A lot of the time, that's around about stability, ah, and secondarily, it is around about addressing the humanitarian issues inside that country. (Interviewee 56, male, Australian government official)

From his experience in the NGO sector in India, Rajput (2019) argues that, disappointingly, some NGOs are also corrupt. Evidence from my sample suggests that Rajput was correct, as attested by Interviewee (36), a senior Catholic priest and an executive in an international organization in Kenya, who argues that even faith-based organizations are not an exception in terms of corruption. This is because, he claims, the issue of corruption in Africa is very complex and hard to resist—even those who claim that they are guided by faith and religious values are not as innocent as they claim (Interviewee 36, male, Catholic priest, and NGO's executive). Consequently, corrupt practices plus the resistance of recipients to accept the contingent cultural demands of the donors discussed here have led to foreign-aid donor fatigue, adversely affecting the scheme's funding and effectiveness in turn.

DONOR FATIGUE AND AID DEPENDENCY

The literature on the history and processes of foreign aid indicates that donor fatigue has affected the effectiveness and delivery of relief and long-term projects in poor countries for a long time. Already three decades ago, in 1990, Ewing and Aldhous (1990, p. 595) suggested that even high-profile intergovernmental organizations such as the WHO faced a funding crisis for their global HIV/AIDS programs because of donor fatigue. In the 1990–91 financial year alone, the organization registered a 30 percent decline in pledged donations, a shortfall that affected all aspects of their programs (Ewing & Aldhous 1990, p. 595). These declining trends have continued ever since. In 2009, Grépin (p. 75) indicated that the rate of donor funding had slowed down in the previous years, falling below the levels required to sustain the HIV programs and to achieve universal access to treatment. Grépin argues that these trends were accentuated by increasing pressure on foreign-aid budgets and donor fatigue. Evidence from my sample suggests that Ewing, Aldhous, and Grépin were correct. Interviewee (29) is a lieutenant general in the army who has commanded troops on the battlefield in Africa, including Somalia, with funding secured through foreign aid. He understands the international community's frustration. However, he warns that the discontinuation from foreign aid and other collective initiatives can have dire consequences globally. Using the Somali case as an example, he claims:

> Let me give an example of Somalia. It is looks like the international community has fatigue. There is a kind of fatigue there. They are tired. However, if they give up and leave all the work to the African countries or Somalia, this will become an international burden. It will be a global problem [. . .]. All terrorist groups are inter-linked. (Interviewee 29, male, lieutenant general in the army)

Despite aid fatigue in the Global North, Gulrajania and Swiss (2019, p. 348) suggest, new non-traditional donors have emerged. These new donors are motivated by their desire to boost their status in the international order as advanced, influential, and sufficiently wealthy to be donor-states. Their donations are, therefore, not out of the kindness of their hearts but for instrumental advancement purposes. On the other hand, Inderfurth, Fabrycky, and Cohen (2005) argued that the level of engagement by the international community depends on the actual crisis' media coverage and, most importantly, the identity of the target and vulnerable population. For example, they claim the huge media coverage of the Indian Ocean tsunami that struck in December 2004, coupled with the fact that a significant number of victims originated from Western countries, resulted in the UN appeal being financed at more than 80 percent within days. Over USD13 billion was raised internationally, with at least 92 countries taking part. The trends were not the same with the earthquake crisis in Pakistan. The disregard of the Pakistan crisis by the international community is not necessarily caused by foreign-aid donor fatigue but, it is suggested, the identity of the vulnerable target populations (Inderfurth, Fabrycky & Cohen 2005). Evidence from my sample indicates they were correct, with Interviewee (48) stating that

> In the former Yugoslavia, then Europeans had a real ownership. It was happening in our backyard. And here, we are now kind of trying to implement ideas from our own experience and for us, the hardest part is to translate that, for example, into the African context. (Interviewee 48, male, colonel in the army and expatriate)

William Easterly (2009, p. 374) writes that saving Africa from poverty has been at the top of several Western countries' foreign policies for years. For example, the members of the 2008 G8 Summit in Japan firmly committed to fulfilling their commitments on the Official Development Assistance, and that included increasing aid to Africa by USD25 billion a year by 2010. However, the continent remains poor (Moyo 2017). Wamboye, Adekola, and Sergi (2014, p. 335) suggest that, while foreign development assistance can be credited for being the largest source of funding for many domestic programs in poor countries, it is held to lead to dependency. They further suggest that the African case is unique. Asian countries that once were at the same income level as some African countries have now emerged, leaving Africa lagging as the continent has failed to wean itself off foreign aid. This is a position they share with Dambisa Moyo (as cited in Kasbaoui & Nechad 2018, p. 133), who suggests that foreign aid to Africa does not make any difference and that, if anything, it makes the situation worse because foreign aid to Africa leads to dependency and perpetual poverty. Gaven Mooney (2009, p. 397) has completely different views, arguing that Moyo's suggestions are not only wrong, but also dangerous for the health and well-being of the average African who depend on foreign aid for survival.

While evidence from my sample here strongly supports the suggestion that foreign aid can be the only means of survival for the poorest of the poor; hence, it remains an important tool to alleviate pressure on the most vulnerable communities in Kenya, it also indicates that Moyo, Wamboye, Adekola, and Sergi were correct to some extent, particularly on the issue of dependency and Africa continuing to lag economically despite a huge amount of money invested in the continent. Interviewee (9) has administered foreign aid locally for many years, including at the time of this interview, and yet, he questions the effectiveness of the scheme.

> Let me explain that, since we gained independence in Africa, we are under foreign aid. Are we moving [forward] because of foreign aid? Are we given the right solutions? The good solutions because of foreign aid or it is just [that] we are given fishes [fish] without being taught how to fish? (Interviewee 9, male, colonel in the army)

But does Africa have what it takes to wean itself off foreign aid? As the Chinese folk saying explains, "if you want to get rich, you build roads first." This is because there is a positive relationship between infrastructure and economic development (Wethal 2019, p. 474). Poor infrastructure prevents African actors from producing and exporting goods and services (Zhang 2010, p. 502). Such conditions affect most of the critical sectors from health, energy, education, and transport to communication, causing sluggish economic growth and plunging the continent into a cycle of poverty (Kuada 2013). For example, Kenyan transport structural gaps remain a serious handicap to growth and poverty reduction (Isaac 2019, p. 200). Similarly, while some efforts have been made to improve the technology sector, the basic systems for leveraging these initiatives in Africa remain fragmented and uncoordinated (Kuada 2013). Evidence from my sample does not reject these assumptions, but it suggests that the African case is a particularly egregious problem and therefore, improving infrastructure alone might not necessarily translate into improved overall performance. For example, Kenyans' mindset has rendered previous development initiatives redundant. Interviewee (7) gives an example:

> I think it was 2002 when the NARC [the National Rainbow Coalition] government came in. They demolished part of Kibera, and they put up high-rise building . . . and the people who were given those houses rented the houses to the middle-level income earners, and they went back to the slums. So, they became landlords. (Interviewee 7, female, NGO's executive)

Interviewee (55) is of a similar view as Interviewee (7). She indicates that the level of education and general understanding in some Kenyan communities is so low that any initiative requires extensive promotional campaigns to succeed. Several projects have, historically, been wasteful. She gives an example of what happened in Nyanza when a foreign-aid-funded organization was working to help locals fight against malaria because the disease was getting out of control due to Lake Victoria. They came in and gave people mosquito nets, free of charge. Two things happened: People did not use the nets, or they used them to catch fish from the lake (Voice 055, Female, Lawyer). The literature and findings presented here show that Africa has failed to achieve a satisfactory level of development and that's why the continent remains dependent on foreign aid, a scheme whose productivity is largely plagued with complex and ineffective administrative and bureaucratic processes.

ADMINISTRATION COSTS, BUREAUCRACY, AND PROCESSES OF FOREIGN AID

Bureaucracy fails domestic and international institutions' efforts to dispense foreign aid equitably. The scheme's structures and processes are designed in a way that beneficiaries have no power. They have limited channels to provide feedback, and even if they did, there are no mechanisms to hold the powerful foreign-aid executives accountable for system failure (Easterly 2002, p. 244). Besides, the complex bureaucratic processes in Kenya create a contrast between the international non-governmental organizations' (INGO) written agenda and their actual practices in the field due to multiple influences from various players with contradicting interests. For instance, INGOs in Kenya must meet the conditions imposed by both the donor and the Kenyan governments, creating significant implementation gaps at the expense of the beneficiaries (Dyke et al. 2014, p. 86). There are multiple decision makers involved in the foreign-aid scheme, making the whole process lengthy, complex, and unproductive because of the conflicting values between governments, INGOs, locally based implementing organizations, and beneficiaries (Martinez 2016, p. 19). Evidence from my sample suggests that Easterly and Martinez as well as Dyke et al. were correct, with Interviewee (41) arguing that even host governments are often too scared to hold NGOs operating within their territorial boundaries to account.

> So, if they come in as saviours; and they are non-governmental organisations; they are implementors of foreign aid because the government, in a way, has failed to manage those funds properly. So, there is a way in which the government can say, "Well, we better not criticise what NGOs are doing because, otherwise, we lose out on this complementary work that NGOs are doing." (Interviewee 41, Catholic priest and academic)

The lack of direct connection between the donor and the implementing partners implies that governments rely on intermediary grant managers who work on the frontlines of global development to monitor, implement, and report on projects in poor countries. For example, the Development Alternatives Incorporated (DAI) accumulated around USD650 million in 2016 alone to work on projects in healthcare, democracy, governance, and economic growth in Africa, Asia, the Middle East, and Latin America, employing 4,000 staff around the world (Indo Asian News Service 2018). Evidence from my sample confirms these practices. Interviewee's (1) organization receives money from foreign governments' agencies. Here, he shares his experience:

> Currently, donors have people that they call grant managers [. . .]. So, if I am having money from Australian Aid, then they will give this money to either DAI [Development Alternative, Inc.], you know [inaudible]. So, if [the] Australian government wants to implement a program in Kenya, whichever, it doesn't matter, whether in health, whether in WASH [Water, Sanitation and Hygiene], whether in agriculture, whether in peace and security, whether in governance or whatever we do, that money will be given to some of these international companies, they call them grant managers. Now these will then look for implementing partners. (Interviewee 1, male, economist, and civil society activist)

On top of millions of dollars wasted in bureaucracy and adverse processes, a large sum of money donated to NGOs goes to administration costs, including big salaries to senior executives. In his paper, Daniel Pollack (2011, p. 600) suggests that the international social work community needs to look in the mirror. There is growing evidence that NGOs have discrepancies between top and bottom salaries that are just as stark as those in the banking sector. The divergence between executive salaries and that of a regular employee has grown dramatically over the past decades, putting NGOs' moral values on the spot. Some of the senior officials in international organizations have annual salaries of more than 500,000 euros (Pollack 2011, p. 600). Evidence from my sample confirms Pollack's argument. The findings here establish that, further to the loss of time, a large amount of money donated to NGOs is used to cover big salaries of senior executives, as Interviewee (2), an economist and activist, attests:

> The way internationals [expatriates] are paid and the way we are paid, it's immoral [. . .]. Somebody is called a volunteer from Australia or UK or wherever, and they live like a minister here, and sometimes, the level of expertise they are bringing is very low [. . .], and the next salary of a black person here is maybe ten times [lower] than the salary of that volunteer. So, the money goes back. (Interviewee 2, male, economist, and civil society activist)

Evidence such as the comment made by my Interviewee (44) further suggests that NGOs spend a lot of money running meetings in luxurious hotels, undermining frontline services delivery in turn. Furthermore, according to

Interviewee (38), a significant amount of money donated to NGOs is used to fund their executives' luxurious lifestyle in Kenya, including using very expensive transport. Their children are educated expensively, and for that reasons, Interviewee (38) believes, 80 percent of the funds are spent on those pretending to help instead of the vulnerable. It is true some vulnerable communities somehow benefit, but the head of the organization often profits more than the beneficiaries in terms of foreign aid (Interviewee 38, male, primary school teacher).

On the other hand, Rezaul Islam's (2014, p. 193) study analyzed NGOs' community empowerment projects in Bangladesh, which does not limit the geographical scope of his findings that can be generalized to what is happening in other parts of the world. Islam's argument that the lack of consultation practically means that the beneficiaries are refused a space in the development processes, preventing them from securing any type of ownership, was tested and proven correct through accounts from my Kenyan sample. The lack of consultation implies that NGOs' activities toward community empowerment of vulnerable Kenyans have had a limited impact. However, despite some disparities, bypass theory postulates that the funding NGOs deliver to relief services directly in the affected communities has ensured vulnerable people's survival (Dietrich 2016, p. 67).

Chapter 5

Bypass Theory

An Effective Way to Prevent Foreign Aid's Capture in Bad Governance and Corruptive Practices

Using bypass theory, chapter 5 examines the positives of foreign aid's history and processes in Kenya. Bypass theory suggests that bypassing governments yields more positive results in terms of foreign-aid effectiveness (Dietrich 2016, p. 67). It is based on evidence that bilateral aid to developing countries leads to unproductive situations where aid goes to waste due to corruption and partially failed systems. Applying bypass theory has influenced some donor governments to change their tactics (Dietrich 2016, p. 67). The theory implies that donor governments give aid funding to non-state actors operating in the field. This way, they reduce the risk of aid capture in bad governance and corruptive environments. Recent evaluations in Kenya have concluded that NGOs-administered aid has seen school programs perform better, leading to overall good outcomes in the education sector (Dietrich 2016, p. 67). Evidence from my sample suggests the ideas suggested by bypass theory are critical, with Interviewee (55) explaining that, with the current system, administrators of aid channeled through Kenyan government will always find a way to misuse funds. She gives an example:

> The National Youth Service is . . . they recruit young people, and they train them in like basic livelihood projects, and they release them. They have a training college somewhere in the Rift Valley. As for the budget of the centre, the budget of this college had people [and] every person enrolled into that college eating two cows in a day. (Interviewee 55, female, lawyer)

Speaking from a donor's perspectives, Interviewee (56) suggests that funding NGOs makes it possible to hold the relevant stakeholders to account, avoiding funds being captured in bad governance and corruption. The same cannot be done with a foreign government. But the success of bypass theory can also partially be explained by NGOs being founded on the idea of volunteerism and humanitarianism. While their work is not perfect, their value setting has made it possible to ease pressure within the most vulnerable communities and systems (Rajput 2019).

Non-governmental organizations' work has also assisted nations overcome several shortfalls, with leadership and management skills that extend to the grassroots levels (Rajput 2019). NGOs' initiatives have been complementary in Kenya, assisting the government to meet the needs of the most vulnerable community members, such as those living with HIV/AIDS. The NGO sector has continued to grow due to the popular policy agenda adopted by major international donors to increase funding opportunities for NGOs rather than governments (Hershey 2013, p. 671). The Kenyan civil society organizations, which are independent and separate from the machinery of the state, benefit from this policy direction and are thriving (Taka & Northey 2020, p. 2), as demonstrated through the literature and findings *below*.

THE IMPACT OF CIVIL SOCIETY ORGANIZATIONS

Bypass theory is credited for the robust nature of the Kenyan civil society organizations (CSOs). Unver et al. (2020) claim that, unlike NGOs, CSOs are not necessarily registered with the government or linked with local markets. This position gives them more freedom and flexibility as they carry out their advocacy work. CSOs include professional associations, universities, and other organizations that usually play an important role in improving local ownership and development. Marita et al. (2016, p. 2) make the same claim that CSOs play a vital role in social, political, and economic development in regional, sub-regional, national, and local processes, enhancing governance and transparency. They argue that such improvements have helped to hold the government accountable as CSOs have the comparative advantage of non-bureaucratized structures. Marita et al.'s arguments align with Miho Taka and Jessica Ayesha Northey's (2020, p. 2) views suggesting that, with the recent oil discovery in Kenya, the capacity and resilience of Kenyan CSOs are more important than ever before. Several participants in my study agree with Unver et al., Marita et al., as well as Taka and Northey. Speaking from her lived experience and observations, Interviewee (55) suggests that foreign-aid funding to the Kenyan civil society has helped to hold the government to account, as she puts it:

> They [organisations] help significantly in governance, particularly in holding the government to account [. . .]. And I think we have the better developed civil

> societies in the region. So, to that extent, definitely, keep the donor funding. (Interviewee 55, female, lawyer)

Similarly, Interviewee (13), an NGO executive and advocate for the rights of urban refugees in Nairobi, argues that thanks to advocacy by NGOs and the civil society, the refugees' rights have improved significantly. She claims that "when it comes to health of refugees, with the help of UNHCR and agencies, refugees currently enjoy the minimum national health insurance. This was also a great achievement" (Interviewee 13, female, expatriate). The point made by Interviewee (13) supports Taka and Northey's (2020, p. 2) argument that Kenyan civil society groups have historically shaped the policy formulations and processes, leading to positive outcomes in terms of the legislation and management of the country's resources. A similar point is made by Wangui Kimari (2018, p. 1), who argues that activists in the poorest areas in Nairobi successfully demand access to vital resources such as water, sanitation, and an end to the extrajudicial killings and police brutality that currently take place, and based on evidence from my sample, Taka and Northey, as well as Kimari, were correct. Interviewee (7), for example, makes a point that CSOs have empowered Kenyans in a way that puts them in a good position to know and stand for their rights.

> They made Kenyans more aware of their rights—community empowerment, yeah. They made Kenyans more [aware]. If you talk about our rights, they are more aware. If you talk about social accountability, which also impacts the amounts that we are being given, people are getting more and more involved. (Interviewee 7, female, NGO's executive)

CSOs' initiatives increase community awareness in terms of rights and responsibility, and this flows on in a chain to other successes. Besides, Claire Mercer (2016, p. 7) suggests that NGOs strengthen the civil society through their activities, which support democratic processes in turn. Therefore, a strong civil society is vital to prevent the state's misuse of power. On the other hand, Mercer (2016, p. 7) further suggests that CSOs can help legitimize the authority of the state when it is based on the rule of law. Similarly, Thomas Obel Hansen and Chandra Lekha Sriram (2015, p. 407) argue that the Kenyan civil society has advanced accountability for serious international crimes, especially during the 2007–08 post-election violence, making the sector the defender and promoter of the norms of accountability at home and abroad. Participants in my study are of similar but grudging views, where they suggest that even if the freedom of expression in Kenya is a great start, it does not necessarily trigger relevant action from the authorities. Interviewee (41) explains:

> I hate to use the word "voiceless" because people cry out, and speak, and their very lives are crying out, but nobody is listening. It is not as if they don't have voices, they have a voice, but maybe somebody somewhere is deaf. (Interviewee 41, Catholic priest and academic)

The robust nature and advocacy of CSOs in Kenya has seen the abolition of a range of discriminatory laws. Interviewee (13) gives the recently secured refugees' freedom of movement as an example, suggesting that even when it comes to moving, it's no longer the case that refugees must be restricted in the camp. They've seen these discriminatory laws falling one after another (Interviewee 13, female, expatriate). Indeed, CSOs and NGOs work in concert to maximize the outcomes for the most vulnerable communities in Kenya, as evidenced in the following section.

THE IMPACT OF NON-GOVERNMENTAL ORGANIZATIONS (NGOS)

The ongoing global humanitarian crisis is a result of natural disasters, diseases, violent conflicts, and other economic and social factors that have led to a cycle of complex emergencies (Aebischer et al. 2017). Governments, faced with the scarcity of resources, rely on NGOs to respond to crises such as the refugee burden. The first refugee influx to Kenya occurred in the 1970s with Ugandans and Ethiopians escaping from political persecutions, gross violations of human rights, and violent conflicts (Mogire 2009, p. 16). Roughly two decades later, 7,000 South Sudanese boys, commonly known as "the lost boys of South Sudan," walked over into Kenya in 1991. At the same time, a large inflow of Somali refugees occurred, forcing Kenya to implement the encampment strategy and handing over the responsibility to UNHCR to screen and ensure their protection and livelihood (Alix-Garcia et al. 2018, p. 67).

The work carried out by UNHCR in Kenya is incredible and complex in nature. On top of hundreds of thousands of refugees living in the camps, there are more than 50,000 urban refugees and asylum seekers in the capital city of Nairobi alone (Balakian 2016, p. 88). As per July 2020, UNHCR Kenya was responsible for the protection of 494,289 refugees and asylum seekers mainly from Somalia, South Sudan, DRC, Ethiopia, Sudan, Rwanda, Eritrea, Burundi, and Uganda (UNHCR 2020b). Other organizations such as the Jesuit Refugee Services (JRS) also work closely with UNHCR to provide short- and long-term services to refugees including, but not limited to, education (Crea & McFarland 2015, p. 237). The education project run by JRS has seen refugees who would otherwise miss out on tertiary education fulfill their dreams (Crea & McFarland 2015, p. 237).

The refugees' living conditions are such that they entirely rely on NGOs for survival. NGOs also provide health, food, water, shelter, and other services these refugees need to survive during their stay in the country. To avoid duplication of services, NGOs divide relief services tasks among themselves. Some take on education and health services, while others oversee food distributions and other needs (Kiura 2014, p. 148). Evidence from my sample aligns with this part of the current literature. Interviewee (49) is a relief and emergency services project officer who has been working with refugees and other vulnerable groups in Kenya for many years. She claims that the work foreign-aid-funded NGOs do with refugees saves their lives.

> Refugees also come under our relief [program] because these are people who are coming to a country without anything, and they just need support. [. . .] For refugees, it is always almost the same—food, clothing and, maybe, health. (Interviewee 49, female, NGO's staff, and former government official)

While corruption within the foreign-aid scheme is historical, there have been positive changes throughout recent years thanks to a political climate that increasingly questions the legitimacy of development assistance. Donors are also under pressure to better control how their money is spent (Dávid-Barrett, Fazekas, Hellmann, Márk & McCorley 2020, p. 481). Above all, Kenyan-based foreign-aid administrators are currently more aware of the realities on the field. For example, Terada, Evans and Mwaniki (2017, p. 52) claim that services allocated to refugees in Turkana County created inequalities between refugees and the host communities in terms of physical infrastructure and economic opportunities. Evidence from my sample suggests that they were correct because this was the case, and collaborations between donors, the Kenyan government, and NGOs were needed to redesign the camps and service delivery models in a way that the locals also benefited. Interviewee (36) explains how the accommodation of the host communities' needs was practically achieved:

> There is always 10–15 percent of our budget [that] goes to the host community, which is the poorest of the poor. Yeah. So, in some instances, you may find that refugees do much better than the host community members. So, out of this concern, for the last few years, we have decided to also include, in our budget, the host community members who are desperate, who equally need support. (Interviewee 36, Catholic priest, and NGO's executive)

On the other hand, Moyer, Sinclair and Spaling (2012) write that faith-based organizations play a key role in bringing about positive changes in the Global South due to their holistic nature, the trust they have earned, and their rootedness in the community. They claim that church groups facilitate the engagement and empowerment of the locals with a deep focus on the values and ethics, and combine the material and the spiritual in a unique way that enhances moral leadership and critical voices. Interviewee (24) confirms these claims, suggesting that faith-based organizations such as the JRS usually go where others are not willing to go, as he puts it:

> JRS started working in Kenya, I think, early 1990s and mostly they have been working in livelihood, ah, education and psycho-social [areas]. [. . .] its slogan . . . may not be written, but "JRS always goes where others do not go." (Interviewee 24, male, NGO's frontline staff)

Faith-based organizations reshape individuals' mindsets and behavior, introducing hope to often demoralized relief workers and residents (Moyer, Sinclair & Spaling's 2012). In the Kibera Slum, Gregory Deacon (2012, p. 664) suggests that life is quite difficult. Kibera's workers and residents' hope has been restored by NGOs, including faith-based organizations, which provide services in health, education, shelter, and a range of long-term projects designed to equip them with the necessary skills to achieve meaningful employment and attitude changes, and evidence from my sample indicates that Moyer, Sinclair, and Spalling as well as Deacon were correct. On the question of "what would happen to the most vulnerable members of the society if NGOs did not exit," Interviewee (32), a poor Kenyan who once lived in Kibera Slum, in his own words, claims that

> It would be extremely hard for people. I am sure a lot of people would have lost their life because, for example, people give birth outside the hospital system. However, NGOs are there, and even providing free services. So, Kibera would be in very bad shape. (Interviewee 32, male, watchman)

The international community has recently reshaped its engagement model in poor countries, increasing support for preventive initiatives. Nibal Zgheib (2020) indicates that international organizations and the European Bank for Reconstruction and Development, for example, joined to empower the Kenyan community with knowledge and skills to boost their preparedness as the coronavirus pandemic continued to evolve. Besides, Kaime-Atterhög, Persson and Ahlberg (2017, p. 580) write that NGOs save the lives of many vulnerable communities, including homeless people and street children in urban areas where they provide outreach, preventive, and remedial interventions designed to improve their welfare. Statements made by my participants support Kaime-Atterhög, Persson, and Ahlberg's claims as well as the content in Zgheib's report. Pleasantly surprised by the reduced number of street children in Nairobi compared to his previous experience, the researcher asked Interviewee (34), whose embassy office is right in the middle of the town, what she believes has happened. She explained that there used to be many in the early 2000s. However, there are currently charity associations that got together and helped street children reintegrate into normal life through training and rehabilitation. Some even reintegrated into schools to gain education, and this has helped phase out life in the streets (Interviewee 34, female, diplomat). Interviewee (49) is of the same views as Interviewee (34). She suggests that faith-based organizations have made a significant contribution to getting children off the streets in Kenya.

> The church has also tried. There are homes that take in street children. We have the Don Bosco Missions—missionaries who are taking the street children. We also have other different missionaries who have home, and they are taking in street boys and street girls. (Interviewee 49, female, NGO's staff, and former government official)

On a larger scale, NGOs have complemented the Kenyan government's work in key areas. Nupur Kukrety and Sumananjali Mohanty (2011, p. 273) claim that NGOs such as Oxfam have helped the Kenyan government to promote gender equality for decades, helping address social injustice and achieve economic leadership for women. My findings establish that Kukrety and Mohanty were correct. Interviewee (11) knows that NGOs initiate and implement projects that have progressively reduced gender imbalance in Kenya. She gives an example of an initiative called "*girl child project*," which was designed to empower girls and women in communities where their rights are undermined. These were communities where, for example, gender mutilations were still practiced, on top of early and forced marriages. With this initiative, a girl child now can go to school and explore her potential (Interviewee 11, female, NGO's frontline staff). Furthermore, Foster, McSorley, and Willetts (2019) claim that Oxfam has lent a helping hand to the most vulnerable Kenyans in terms of water supply and related technologies. By early 2016, around 100 water BluePumps had been installed in Turkana and most of these were installed by Oxfam Kenya, with a robust design that can lift groundwater from a range of depths. Evidence from my sample establishes that Foster, McSorley and Willetts's claims are true, as supported by Interviewee (23), a beneficiary.

> We walked long distances to look for water. Humans, cows, we accessed water from the same place. We drank [water] from the same place, the same time as cows, everything. Goats, sheep, yeah. We fetched the same water [. . .]. It had a lot of implications. Do you know the impacts of drinking such water? It brought a lot of problems to humans. Yeah. [. . .] You know that drink brought diseases [. . .]. This is in the past though. We can now access cleaner water. (Interviewee 23, male, security guard and foreign-aid beneficiary)

Evidently, the interviewees are largely in agreement with the fundamentals of bypass theory in that they see the living conditions of poor Kenyans as having improved. However, this dependence on NGOs and the churches could prevent Kenyan citizens from holding their government to account as part of a democratic need to push authorities to redistribute resources in an uncorrupted fashion. In her interview with Al Jazeera (2018), Dambisa Moyo argued that while African citizens would like to hold their governments to account in terms of the quality of service delivery, they are not able to do so because NGOs are delivering those outcomes. Besides, Khaldoun AbouAssi (2013, p. 585) writes that the overreliance or potentially manipulatable dependence on foreign aid implies that stakeholders on the ground sometimes respond to their donors' interests, not the vulnerable population's needs. Consequently, when donors shift their focus, local NGOs must adjust their programs on the field accordingly, even if the newly established priorities do not align with the needs and values of the vulnerable people. After all, it is not always about the vulnerable beneficiaries, it primarily about foreign-aid administrators' jobs and the big salaries they accumulate. My sample agrees. Interviewee (42) regrets that Kenyans must turn to NGOs for services that are supposed to be the government's responsibility.

> [. . .] I am not going to my government to look for the necessary help I deserve because I am a taxpayer, because I am just a citizen, a member of the community. Instead, I am waiting for World Vision, IMF, . . . Médecins Sans Frontières [French for "Doctors Without Borders"] MSF, to come and help me deal with all these, you know, issues that I am having. No, it shouldn't be that way in the first place. (Interviewee 42, Catholic priest and academic)

Recently, the role and performance of the Kenyan government have improved thanks to the advocacy and pressure from NGOs and CSOs. For example, the Kenyan constitution currently obliges local governments to be aware of and respond to the needs of the citizens. They are also required to ensure public participation in local governance—a great achievement (Fuo 2015, p. 167). Additionally, Kenya currently tries harder to find solutions to its domestic challenges internally. However, knowing that some issues faced by African countries are transnational in nature (Nicoll & Delaney 2010), Kenya and other African nations have no choice but to be a part of collective initiatives through regional and global partnerships, mainly in peace and security, as demonstrated through the following chapter.

REGIONAL AND GLOBAL PARTNERSHIPS

Various reports indicate that regional and global partnerships that have been established to collectively deal with security threats in Africa have been successful. They equip the continent with the resources necessary to boost its overall security. The African Union Mission in Somalia (AMISOM), for example, has made important political and military progress in its effort to eradicate terror threats by Al-Shabaab and other Al-Qaeda-affiliated militants (Schulman & Williams 2012, p. 34). Despite a few challenges, AMISOM had nearly reached its target strength set by the UN Security Council by 2012, with additional contingents committed from Kenya, Djibouti, and Sierra Leone to further support the stalwarts from Uganda and Burundi (Schulman & Williams 2012, p. 34). AMISOM has undergone major evolutions since it was first deployed to Mogadishu in March 2007, growing its area of operation from just a few districts of the capital city of Mogadishu to the whole of South-Central Somalia and expanding its initial force of around 1,600 to over 22,000 troops as per January 2016 (Williams 2016, p. 40).

With the current forces of globalization, conflicts are interconnected and transnational. Knowing that a local problem quickly becomes a global one (Hrubec & Uhde 2018, p. 777), defeating terrorists in Somalia has meant a more stable region. While the international community once favored hard stabilization efforts to destroy Al-Shabaab and Al-Qaeda affiliates in Somalia, a softer and more comprehensive approach that has been combining hard actions and refining population-centric counter-insurgency measures through talks, ad hoc political deals, transitional justice, and reconciliation initiatives has led to better outcomes. This was made possible by defense and intelligence establishments by international actors such as Britain, the United States, the European Union, Norway, and the Netherlands (Gelot 2020, p. 253). The participation of regional and global actors in Somalia makes perfect security and political sense. With the growing concerns over jihadism and its perceived correlation with migration, new strategic partnerships for joint operations designed to promote counterterrorism-inspired stabilization are crucial (Moe & Geis 2020, p. 399).

The evolving sub-regional organizations such as the Common Market for Eastern and Southern Africa (COMESA), Intergovernmental Authority on Development (IGAD), the East African Community (EAC), and the Eastern Africa Standby Force (EASF) have initiated projects where countries work collectively toward the economic, political, and security issues facing the region. They have overlapping membership and mandates, and Kenya is a member of each of these organizations. As regional insecurity has hindered development and integration, member states have developed several state-centric guiding principles to improve the situation (Bayeh 2020, p. 127). The international community provides support to such initiatives, including bolstering training of local police and civilian specialists in armed groups. Major contributors in personnel and funding include the United States, France, Germany, Finland, Norway, Denmark, Japan, and the United Kingdom (Nicoll & Delaney 2010). Evidence from my sample suggests that the literature above is correct, with Interviewee (9), one of the leaders of the EASF, arguing that the African collective efforts were sparked by the need to meet high security threats such as the terrorist threats arising from Somalia.

> We are also addressing the issue at the continental level where [the] African Union came up with AMISON, [that is], African [Union] Mission in Somalia. When we started that mission, Mogadishu was completely controlled by Al-Shabaab. Nowadays, we captured Mogadishu. It is a little bit secured. Then we captured other towns. Now, three quarter[s] of Somali people are controlled by AMISOM and [the Somali] National Security [Forces]. (Interviewee 9, male, colonel in the army)

Whatever the motivation might be, global partnerships have contributed to professional development within the armed and security forces in East Africa, among other achievements. Interviewee (43) is a diplomat and a senior military officer with the rank of colonel. He believes that the monetary, knowledge, and intelligence support from Scandinavian countries has enabled them to fight terrorism from its roots. Interviewee (43) makes a point that these international actors are mainly interested in the fight against terrorism from a distance because, he claims, it is not good for them to start fighting terrorists after they have already arrived on their soil—"get them before they come" (Interviewee 43, male, colonel in the army). Similarly, Interviewee (48), a military advisor from one of the Scandinavian countries, suggests that they are in East Africa to help, and he is satisfied with what they have been able to achieve so far, as he puts it:

> We are planning our activities toward different scenarios and the worst one is, of course, if genocide for example starts somewhere or there are huge natural disasters or war crimes appears or something like that. So, we have been focusing, quite much to the worst-case scenarios. (Interviewee 48, male, colonel in the army and expatriate)

The findings in this section exhibit that regional and global partnerships are important for countries like Kenya as they not only boost their preparedness, but they also contribute to addressing some of the most pressing issues, reducing pressure on people and systems.

Conclusion

Discussions and Recommendations

Factors that shape and influence the impact of foreign aid on human security in Africa have generally received limited scholarly attention in recent history. Kenya was used as a case study to evaluate the effectiveness of the foreign-aid scheme, as a Sub-Saharan African country and major recipient of foreign aid (McCormick & Schmitz 2011, p. 156). Existing scholarly evidence indicates that aid schemes complement the Kenyan government's work, improving its public perception and legitimacy to a certain extent (Dolan 2020, p. 145). But some evidence in this book, for example Moyo's (2017) views, also shows that the effectiveness of foreign aid to alleviate poverty in Africa is generally disputed. This book has outlined the key underlying factors of the scheme's failure to bring about significant and long-term changes in average Kenyans' living standards.

This book has used theories such as bypass to test Dietrich's (2016, p. 67) suggestion that funding NGOs operating in the field instead of governments yields more positive results in terms of measurable outcomes, such as living standards of ordinary Kenyan beneficiaries. For example, several participants in my research that informed this book indicated that foreign-aid funding to the Kenyan civil society has helped to hold the government to account, a move that has significantly increased Kenyans' prospects to wean themselves off foreign aid. My participants' arguments also endorse Taka and Northey's (2020, p. 2) suggestion that, with the recent oil discovery in Kenya, the capacity and resilience of Kenyan civil society organizations were used as a base to empower Kenyans as they fight for their rights and a fairer share. That way, bypass theory suggests aid delivery that provides a transition to long-term solutions, with designs and processes that equip Kenyans with the necessary knowledge, skills, and confidence to become masters of their own destiny.

Human security is particularly relevant in the Kenyan context, where it is crucial for policy makers to think beyond the state as the principal and only actor to be secured, to include the fundamental freedoms that are vital for a dignified human life (Camilleri 2012, p. 12). Similarly, this research has demonstrated that the international community has the responsibility to encourage and assist sovereign states to protect their citizens from current and imminent threats, or to take a collective relevant action where states have, willingly or unwillingly, failed to fulfill their obligations, based on the principles of international law. The existing literature has helped the author of this book to broaden his understanding of key underlying factors shaping and influencing the effectiveness of foreign aid in Kenya.

All Kenyan human security issues identified by the existing literature are complex in nature. However, the most concerning threat facing Kenyan society today is poverty, which essentially shapes all critical sectors affecting Kenyans' lives, including but not limited to food security (Oluoko-Odingo 2011, p. 2). Poverty has also undermined vulnerable Kenyans' prospects for quality education, with Polkovnikova-Wamoto, Mathai, Vander Stoep, and Kumar (2016, p. 286) demonstrating that while education is a great tool for positive change, the high rates of school dropouts in Kenya due to poverty have had an adverse impact on the sector and led to a chain of other vulnerabilities. For example, poverty creates impoverishment in certain aspects of caregiving, compromising general child safety. Children in Kenya, especially those who are homeless in major cities, face issues of compromised development and secure attachment (Polkovnikova-Wamoto et al. 2016, p. 286).

Kenya also suffers from historic internal conflicts and political intolerance. Authors such as Whittaker (2012, p. 391) suggest that even securing independence from British colonial rule in 1963 did not change the colonialist patterns already established. Besides, the country has faced terrorist threats for a long time, putting Kenyans and temporary residents at risk (Tharoor 2015). On the other hand, a range of beliefs and cultural practices put some members of Kenyan communities in a vulnerable position, and practices that might be outdated or immoral by Western standards continue to affect Kenyans' health and well-being today (Machangu 2015, p. 274). The most pressing one is widow inheritance, which contributes to a higher prevalence of HIV/AIDS within the Kenyan female population (Agot et al. 2010, p. e14028). Similarly, Agesa, Agesa and Dabalen (2009, p. 431) demonstrate that there continues to exist a remarkable gender imbalance in Kenyan society. Males possess relatively higher wealth, education, and skills that lead to a significant and justified gender pay gap.

Evidence (Njuguna, Mwangi & Kamau 2014, p. 204) suggests that Kenya faces critical healthcare workforce shortages and that, despite the United Nations Millennium Development Goals' (MDGs) objective to combat poverty, hunger, disease, and a range of other underlying factors of Kenyans' health and well-being, the country remained far from attaining these goals by their desired timeframe of 2015 (Kingery et al. 2016, p. 92) has been tested and proven correct. On top of this comes the pressing issue of poor housing, as demonstrated by Winter, Dzombo and Barchi (2019), who stipulate that housing has become a major hindrance to attaining an acceptable standard of health and well-being in Kenya, particularly in Nairobi where about 60 percent of the population live in informal settlements, the slums. The conditions in slums are deplorable, with poor housing, poor quality water, and poor sanitation (Winter, Dzombo & Barchi 2019).

The literature and accounts from the participants in the research that informed this book graphically show the complexities in Kenyan human security issues, and it is worth investigating the underlying factors, including the legacies of colonial and neo-colonial practices. The adverse consequences of the legacies of colonialism, neo-colonialism, and imperialist practices for Kenyans' health and well-being today have effectively and convincingly been articulated. For example, Hughes (2008, p. 134) points to the historic exploitation of Kenyan natural resources by the British colonial administration that progressively became one of the many grievances in Kenyan villages. Similarly, Waller (2012, p. 05) made a point that actions by the former colonial masters continue to shape Africans' daily life today psychologically, economically, and socially, particularly in relation to land and property rights, while Mwangi (2010, p. 87) argues that the brutality suffered by indigenous Kenyans during their struggle for independence and self-determination, coupled with some key colonial practices such as land alienation, continues to affect them today in a way that impedes their overall performance and delays their material progress. Meier Zu Selhausen and Weisdorf (2016, p. 230) made a similar point that this history largely contributes to the marginalization of African women, for example, in ways that have their roots in earlier colonial practices.

A part of the existing literature rejects the assumption that the British "divide-and-rule" strategy is the sole source of divisions and tensions within Kenyan society. Kenyans have always been divided, it is claimed by most of my sample. For example, Ray (2018, p. 367) argues that the divide-and-rule theory is incomplete and too simplistic, as it assumes that the colonial strategists severely disrupted the pre-colonial political and social trends, rendering the latter irrelevant as we try to understand the current community divisions, and my sample largely agree with Ray on this one. The literature further indicates that East African countries have long been one of the testing grounds for neo-colonialism, whereby their economic and political policies are dictated from outside, by more powerful actors (Maekawa 2015, p. 317), and this has been proven through verbal accounts from my sample.

There also exists a strategic and progressive destruction of African local markets. For example, decades ago, African countries were net food exporters, but almost every African nation has now become a net food importer, with the continent importing about 25 percent of its food because globalized capitalist industrial agriculture has forced emerging countries to integrate into a system where export-oriented production is dominated by large industrial farms, leaving limited room for poor financial performers (Bello 2008, p. 453). The literature also points to a brain drain phenomenon where African governments send students to universities in Western countries hoping that they will come back and contribute, but only a handful of them return to Africa upon completion of their degree programs. This has negative implications for African development (El-Khawas 2005, p. 40), raising the question as to whether Kenya has adequate human resources to help implement policies that could improve the practices and processes within the foreign-aid scheme.

It can be concluded that the effectiveness of foreign aid, or the need to donate to poor countries, remains a controversial topic. However, despite the ongoing controversies about the role of foreign aid in alleviating poverty and other human security issues, the number of donors has increased in recent years to include non-traditional donors (Mawdsley 2010, p. 361). Authors such as Snowdon (2009, p. 247) have argued that any suggestion to increase foreign aid to regions such as Sub-Saharan Africa has historically met strong criticism. The debates around it have always been plagued with issues of causality, measurement, feasibility, politics, and ideologies (Snowdon 2009, p. 247). Similarly, other authors such as Moyo (2017) argue that foreign aid plunges Africa into perpetual poverty and dependence, while William Easterly (2003, p. 25) suggests that foreign aid never reaches the poor who deserve it most because of corruption and other adverse practices. Peter T. Bauer, one of the most vocal critics of foreign aid, once described the foreign-aid process as "a transfer of resources from the taxpayer of a donor country to the Government of a recipient country" (as cited in Shleifer 2009, p. 379). But there are also optimists such as Sachs (2014) and Adedokun (2017, p. 184) who argue that foreign aid is an important tool to alleviate poverty and promote growth. On the other hand, DeBoom (2019, p. 16) suggests that there are concerns in relation to donors' interests in Africa, particularly around the increasing Chinese dominant entry into the continent through their loan schemes. But Wang Yiwei (2018) calls this a Western hypocrisy—the attention on the Chinese debt trap by Western critics leads us to wonder if the West really cares about poor countries' vulnerability to Chinese loans' practices or whether they are simply concerned about their compromised position as they compete for interests in the region, a point shared with Jean-Claude Berthélemy

(2006, p. 179) who argues that Africa is simply a battlefield between the West and the East.

This book has also explored how donor fatigue affects the effectiveness and delivery of relief projects in Africa and beyond, with Ewing and Aldhous (1990, p. 595) suggesting that, already three decades ago in 1990, even high-profile intergovernmental organizations such as the World Health Organization (WHO) faced a funding crisis for their global HIV/AIDS programs because of donor fatigue. Besides et al. (2014, p. 335) made a point that, while foreign aid can be credited with being the largest source of funding for many domestic programs in poor and developing countries, it also leads to dependency. On the other hand, the bureaucracy has failed domestic and international institutions' efforts to dispense foreign aid equitably. This is because the scheme's structures and processes are designed in a way that beneficiaries have no power, making it impossible to drive positive changes at the grassroots level (Easterly 2002, p. 244). Similarly, the lack of a direct connection between the donor and the implementing partners on the field implies that governments rely on costly intermediary grant managers to monitor and report on the progress and feasibility of the projects being funded, negatively affecting the overall outcomes at the beneficiary level due to the time lost and the amount of money wasted as a result (Indo Asian News Service 2018).

Existing literature (Nicoll & Delaney 2010) and accounts from my sample also indicate that projects carried out through regional and global partnerships have empowered local East African actors to effectively deal with pressing issues, especially in peace and security. These projects are partially funded by Western donors. For example, the East African Standby Force's long-term solution is to collectively enhance peace and security in the Eastern African Region by member states; that is, Burundi, Comoros, Djibouti, Ethiopia, Kenya, Rwanda, Seychelles, Somalia, Sudan, and Uganda (EASF 2021) and this is achieved through on-field training and capacity building within the local security and police forces (Nicoll & Delaney 2010).

Several ideas, approaches, and modes of aid delivery have been explored in this book, including bypass theory. Ideas suggested by bypass theory are based on evidence that government-to-government aid results in unproductive situations where aid goes to waste due to corrupt and failed systems. Consequently, some donors have now changed tactics, applying bypass theory and hoping for better outcomes at the grassroots level (Dietrich 2016, p. 67). But existing literature and evidence from my sample do not present unambiguous support of bypass theory. Rather, it shows that both governments and NGOs suffer from corruption, as it can be evidenced through the work of authors such as Moyo (2017) and Wamboye, Adekola and Sergi (2014, p. 335), who argue that foreign aid plunges Africa into perpetual poverty and dependence. William Easterly (2003, p. 25) also makes a point that foreign aid never reaches the poor who deserve it most because of corruption and other adverse practices.

The biggest issue with bypass theory, as uncovered by the existing literature and accounts from my sample, is that its uniform installation could deprive Kenyan citizens of the ability to hold their government to account as demonstrated by Dambisa Moyo, who, during her interview with Al Jazeera (2018), argued that, while African citizens would like to hold their governments to account in terms of the quality of service delivery, they are not able to do so because NGOs are delivering those outcomes. Generally, the literature Marita et al. (2016, p. 2) and participants in my research endorse bypass theory based on the Kenyan experience. They argue that bypassing the Kenyan government by funding NGOs that work directly with beneficiaries has seen improvements in the safety, health, and well-being of average Kenyans.

The methodology in this study was designed to find out what Kenyan citizens and Kenyan residents believe is the impact of foreign aid on human security in their country. Data that has informed this book was secured through qualitative research methodology where locals' original accounts have been triangulated with the material from primary and secondary sources. It brought into sharp focus on the answer to the question, "how does foreign aid affect human security in Kenya?" This methodology appropriately investigated individuals' lived experiences as they were presented through feelings, ideas, perceptions, attitudes, and thoughts (Cf. Öhman 2005, p. 273). The choice of the Republic of Kenya as the research site and Kenyan citizens and residents as the research population was not coincidental. It made data collection and processes relatively less complex because Kenya, as a Sub-Saharan African country and a major recipient of foreign aid (McCormick & Schmitz 2011, p. 156), provided all the opportunities and tools to carry out an investigation on the impact of foreign aid on human security from local and indigenous perspectives, making this research project unique.

RECOMMENDATIONS

NGOs' and CSOs' service delivery leads to community empowerment, helping vulnerable community members achieve a higher level of performance financially, socially, and politically. They also equip them with the skills and knowledge necessary to stand for their own rights and demand a fair share of the country's resources. For example, both my sample and the literature (Oxfam 2017) suggest that international non-governmental organizations (INGOs) such as Oxfam have engaged in peacebuilding and social cohesion projects, actively campaigning for better governance and equity in Kenya for many years, and this has resulted in poverty reduction to a certain extent. That is why most of my sample recommends that international donors adopt methods that are consistent with those ideas to be found in bypass theory because it has made a difference. Several participants in my research came to a similar conclusion that, with several controversies within the NGOs' sector, bypass theory needs some adjustment to consider the reality of the lived experience on the ground. This is of particular importance in this research, which was designed to give Kenyan indigenous populations, Kenyan residents, beneficiaries of foreign aid, and frontline staff a voice. My participants recommend four practical changes in the processes and practices of foreign aid: (1) enhanced consultations and engagement with beneficiaries, (2) enhanced collaborations between key stakeholders, (3) a clearer exit strategy, and (4) more rigorous monitoring to stop corruptive practices.

CONSULTATIONS AND ENGAGEMENT WITH BENEFICIARIES

My sample attests that NGOs and CSOs carry out more consultations with beneficiaries than the Government of Kenya. It also suggests that NGOs and CSOs work more closely with beneficiaries, even if the level of engagement could improve. Islam (2014, p. 193) made a crucial point that the lack of consultation between NGOs and the beneficiaries practically means that beneficiaries are refused a space in the development processes, preventing them from securing any type of ownership. Therefore, some NGOs' activities toward community empowerment of vulnerable people have had a limited impact. This is sometimes the case in Kenya, with my participants, such as Interviewee (25), a beneficiary, suggesting that the lack of consultations impedes overall outcomes simply because NGOs end up opting for wrong interventions, causing massive disengagement by the intended beneficiaries. It is recommended that more and broader consultations are carried out within the target populations first for the implementing partners to fully understand the priorities from the beneficiaries' perspectives and second, for the beneficiaries to secure ownership and a space in the development process. As Interviewee (25) puts it, it should be about them. It is their life.

ENHANCED COLLABORATION BETWEEN STAKEHOLDERS

It is recommended that stakeholders work together to ensure there are no duplications of services and to minimize conflicts of interest. For example, refugees' living conditions are such that they entirely rely on NGOs for survival. A group of stakeholders provide different services in health, food, water, shelter, education, and other services these refugees need to survive during their stay in Kenya. Kiura (2014, p. 148) claims that, to avoid duplication of services, NGOs divide relief services tasks among themselves. Some take on education and health services while others are in charge of food distributions and other needs. But Interviewee (35), a teenager and foreign-aid beneficiary living in Nairobi and others, explained that the duplication of services is still a reality in Kenya. More dangerously, they claim, duplication of services is always coupled with conflicts of interest. As such, they specifically asked the researcher to ensure his recommendations section asks relevant stakeholders to work together because whenever conflicts of interest occur, the weakest in the chain; that is, the beneficiaries suffer as they become the punching bag.

CLEAR EXIT STRATEGY

The sample recommends that NGOs implementing foreign aid projects have a clear exit strategy to avoid chronic dependency. This aligns with Moyo's (as cited in Kasbaoui & Nechad 2018, p. 133) concerns that foreign aid to Africa leads to dependency and perpetual poverty. But my sample is ambivalent, and for most of the part, they also support Gaven Mooney's (2009, p. 397) point that Moyo's suggestions are wrong and dangerous for the health and well-being of the average Africans who depend on foreign aid to survive. Therefore, several participants suggest that NGOs keep doing their work, but they should design clear exit strategies in a way that all projects boost Kenyans' prospects for financial independence and autonomy in the long run. These recommendations practically imply that beneficiaries would like to be supported to a certain extent and be left alone to take control of their life and destiny, with dignity. But evidence from my sample suggests that some NGOs strategically place beneficiaries in vulnerable positions for their organizations to remain relevant because they also engage in corrupt practices such as bribes for services, sexual exploitation, collusion, favoritism in the award of contracts and employment offers, fund mismanagement, and embezzlement (Adebajo 2022) just to name a few.

RIGOROUS MONITORING TO CAPTURE AND STOP CORRUPT PRACTICES

The literature suggests that both government-to-government aid and aid channeled through NGOs and CSOs are subject to corruptive practices. While most of my sample argues that many Kenyans would not survive without foreign aid, it also suggests foreign-aid projects have not made a significant difference at the grassroots level because of the high level of corruption in all Kenyan sectors. As such, my sample recommends more rigorous monitoring of projects being funded to ensure the money donated makes a difference at the beneficiaries' level. They suggest:

- More donors' surprise site visits in Kenya,
- more frequent evaluations and surveys with beneficiaries, not service providers, and
- more rigorous checks of the field reports.

The recommendations above would improve foreign aid practices and processes significantly, enabling vulnerable communities to take control of their own development and improve their conditions in key areas of social justice, human rights, and community empowerment, just to name a few.

Bibliography

AbouAssi, K. 2013. Hands in the pockets of mercurial donors: NGO response to shifting funding priorities. *Nonprofit & Voluntary Sector Quarterly*, *42*(3), 584–602. https://doi.org/10.1177/0899764012439629

Adebajo, K. 2022. The dark reality of corruption, lack of accountability among humanitarian orgs in Africa. *HumAngle*. https://humanglemedia.com/the-dark-reality-of-corruption-lack-of-accountability-among-humanitarian-orgs-in-africa/

Adede, C., Oboko, R., Wagacha, P.W., & Atzberger, C. 2019. A mixed model approach to vegetation condition prediction using Artificial Neural Networks (ANN): Case of Kenya's operational drought monitoring. *Remote Sensing*, *11*(9), 1099. https://doi.org/10.3390/rs11091099

Adedokun, A.J. 2017. Foreign aid, governance and economic growth in Sub-Saharan Africa: Does one cap fit all? *African Development Review*, *29*(2), 184–196.

Adekoya, A.F., & Razak, N.A.A. 2016. Effect of crime on poverty in Nigeria. *Romanian Economic & Business Review*, *11*(2), 30.

Adelman, H. 2002. Theory and humanitarian intervention. In M. Keren & D.A. Sylvan (eds.), *International Intervention: Sovereignty Versus Responsibility*. London, Portland: Frank Cass & Co. Ltd., pp. 3–26.

Adesote, S.A., & Osunkoya, O.A. 2018. The brain drain, skilled labour migration and its impact on Africa's development, 1990s–2000s. *Journal of Pan African Studies*, *12*(1), 395–420.

Aebischer Perone, S., Martinez, E., du Mortier, S., Rossi, R., Pahud, M., Urbaniak, V., Chappuis, F., Hagon, O., Jacquérioz Bausch, F., & Beran, D. 2017. Non-communicable diseases in humanitarian settings: Ten essential questions. *Conflict & Health*, *11*(1), 17–11. https://doi.org/10.1186/s13031-017-0119-8

Agensky, J.C. 2020. Who governs? Religion and order in postcolonial Africa. *Third World Quarterly*, *41*(4), 583–602. https://doi.org/10.1080/01436597.2019.1700791

Agesa, R.U., Agesa, J., & Dabalen, A. 2009. Changes in wage distributions, wage gaps and wage inequality by gender in Kenya. *Journal of African Economies*, *18*(3), 431–460. https://doi.org/10.1093/jae/ejn023

Agot, K.E., Stoep, A.V., Tracy, M., Obare, B.A., Bukusi, E.A., Ndinya-Achola, J.O., Moses, S., & Weiss, N.S. 2010. Widow inheritance and HIV prevalence in Bondo district, Kenya: Baseline results from a prospective cohort study. *PLoS One*, *5*(11), e14028. https://doi.org/10.1371/journal.pone.0014028

Agyepong, I.A., Sewankambo, N., Binagwaho, A., Coll-Seck, A.M., Corrah, T., Ezeh, A., . . . Piot, P. 2017. The path to longer and healthier lives for all Africans by 2030: The Lancet commission on the future of health in Sub-Saharan Africa. *The Lancet (British Edition)*, *390*(10114), 2803–2859. https://doi.org/10.1016/s0140-6736(17)31509-x

Al Jazeera. 2009. Kenyan witch-hunt targets elders. *Al Jazeera News*. https://www.aljazeera.com/news/africa/2009/12/2009122683921769977.html

Al Jazeera. 2018. Dambisa Moyo: Foreign aid is 'corrosive' to democracy in Africa. *Al Jazeera News*. https://www.aljazeera.com/news/2018/08/dambisa-moyo-foreign-aid-corrosive-democracy-africa-180802105756584.html

Alberts, H.C. 2007. Beyond the headlines: Changing patterns in international student enrollment in the United States. *GeoJournal*, *68*(2–3), 141–153. https://doi.org/10.1007/s10708-007-9079-7

Alix-Garcia, J., Walker, S., Bartlett, A., Onder, H., & Sanghi, A. 2018. Do refugee camps help or hurt hosts? The case of Kakuma, Kenya. *Journal of Development Economics*, *130*, 66–83. https://doi.org/10.1016/j.jdeveco.2017.09.005

Allen, R.C. 2011. Why the industrial revolution was British: Commerce, induced invention, and the scientific revolution. *The Economic History Review*, *64*(2), 357–384. https://doi.org/10.1111/j.1468-0289.2010.00532.x

Anyangwe, E. 2017. Why is Africa so poor? You asked Google—here's the answer. *The Guardian*. https://www.theguardian.com/commentisfree/2017/jun/28/why-africa-so-poor-google

Anyanwu, J.C. 2014. Oil wealth, ethno-religious-linguistic fractionalization and civil wars in Africa: Cross-country evidence. *African Development Review*, *26*(2), 209–236. https://doi.org/10.1111/1467-8268.12077

Auchter, J. 2017. Forced male circumcision: Gender-based violence in Kenya. *International Affairs*, *93*(6), 1339–1356. https://doi.org/10.1093/ia/iix183

Auerswald, C., Kwena, Z.A., Ochieng, J.H., & Bukusi, E.A. 2012. Life cycle of street children in Kisumu, Kenya. *Journal of Adolescent Health*, *50*(2), S5. https://doi.org/10.1016/j.jadohealth.2011.10.029

Ayodeji, G.I., & Tobi, A.A. 2019. Grand corruption in Sub-Saharan Africa and feasibility of establishing international anti-corruption court. *Acta Universitatis Danubius. Administratio*, *11*(1), 5–24.

Balakian, S. 2016. "Money is your government": Refugees, mobility, and unstable documents in Kenya's operation Usalama watch. *African Studies Review*, *59*(2), 87–111. https://doi.org/10.1017/asr.2016.36

Baloyi, E. 2015. The Christian church's role in the escalating mob justice system in our black townships—An African pastoral view. *Hervormde Teologiese Studies*, *71*(2), 1–7. https://doi.org/10.4102/hts.v71i2.2833

Bar, J. 2016. The problem of Islamic terrorism in Kenya in terms of regional security in East Africa. *Politeja—Pismo Wydzialu Studiow Miedzynarodowych i Politycznych Uniwersytetu Jagiellonskiego*, *13*(42), 147–164.

Barakabitze, A.A., William-Andey Lazaro, A., Ainea, N., Mkwizu, M.H., Maziku, H., Matofali, A.X., Iddi, A., & Sanga, C. 2019. Transforming African education systems in science, technology, engineering, and mathematics (STEM) using ICTs: Challenges and opportunities. *Education Research International*, *2019*, 1–29. https://doi.org/10.1155/2019/6946809

Barbour, B., & Gorlick, B. 2008. Embracing the 'responsibility to protect': A repertoire of measures including asylum for potential victims. *International Journal of Refugee Law*, *20*(4), 533–566. https://doi.org/10.1093/ijrl/een035

Barnett, J., & Adger, W.N. 2007. Climate change, human security and violent conflict. *Political Geography*, *26*(6), 639–655. https://doi.org/10.1016/j.polgeo.2007.03.003

Bataka, H. 2020. Globalization and gender inequality in Sub-Saharan Africa. *The International Trade Journal*, *34*(6), 516–534.

Bauer, P.T. 1974. Foreign aid: Reply to two critics. *Millennium: Journal of International Studies*, *3*(2), 169–172. https://doi.org/10.1177/03058298740030020701

Bayeh, E. 2020. The proliferation of overlapping sub-regional organisations in Eastern Africa: An opportunity for or a challenge to the security of the region? *African Studies (Johannesburg)*, *79*(1), 125–142. https://doi.org/10.1080/00020184.2020.1755828

BBC. 2013. *Mau Mau torture victims to receive compensation – Hague*. https://www.bbc.com/news/uk-22790037

BBC News. 2013. Westgate mall attack in 60 seconds. *BBC*. https://www.bbc.com/news/av/world-africa-29247163

BBC News. 2019a. Rwanda genocide: 100 days of slaughter. *BBC*. https://www.bbc.com/news/world-africa-26875506

BBC News. 2019b. Kenya attack: Nine arrests over bloody DusitD2 hotel siege. *BBC*. https://www.bbc.com/news/world-africa-46902564

Behnam, B., Azimi, F., & Kanani, A.B. 2017 Slave-master relationship and postcolonial translation and teaching. *Journal of Language Teaching & Research*, *8*(3), 565. https://doi.org/10.17507/jltr.0803.15

Bello, W. 2008. How to manufacture a global food crisis. *Development*, *51*(4), 450–455. https://doi.org/10.1057/dev.2008.60

Benoit, C., Jansson, M., Millar, A., & Phillips, R. 2005. Community-academic research on hard-to-reach populations: Benefits and challenges. *Qualitative Health Research*, *15*(2), 263–282.

Berthélemy, J. 2006. Bilateral donors' interest vs. recipients' development motives in aid allocation: Do all donors behave the same? *Review of Development Economics*, *10*(2), 179–194. https://doi.org/10.1111/j.1467-9361.2006.00311.x

Beyene, H.G. 2015. Are African diasporas development partners, peace-makers or spoilers? The case of Ethiopia, Kenya and Nigeria. *Diaspora Studies*, *8*(2), 145–161. https://doi.org/10.1080/09739572.2015.1029714

Bhattacharya, J. 2019. The story of Indian business: The great transition into the new millennium. *Association of Asian Studies*, *24*(2), 22–27.

Bloom, H. 2007. *Bloom modern critical views*. New York: Infobase Publishing, p. 4.

Boye, S.R., & Kaarhus, R. 2011. Competing claims and contested boundaries: Legitimating land rights in Isiolo District, Northern Kenya. *Africa Spectrum*, *46*(2), 99–124.

Brautigam, D., & Rithmire, M. 2021. The Chinese 'Dept Trap' is a myth. *The Atlantic*. https://www.theatlantic.com/international/archive/2021/02/china-debt-trap-diplomacy/617953/

Brech, V., & Potrafke, N. 2014. Donor ideology and types of foreign aid. *Journal of Comparative Economics*, *42*(1), 61–75. https://doi.org/10.1016/j.jce.2013.07.002

Broughton, A. 2018. How imperialism maintains poverty in Africa. *Green Left Weekly*. https://www.greenleft.org.au/content/how-imperialism-maintains-poverty-africa

Brown, S., & Raddatz, R. 2014. Dire consequences or empty threats? Western pressure for peace, justice and democracy in Kenya. *Journal of Eastern African Studies*, *8*(1), 43–62. https://doi.org/10.1080/17531055.2013.869008

Burdine, J.T., Thorne, S., & Sandhu, G. 2021. Interpretive description: A flexible qualitative methodology for medical education research. *Medical Education*, *55*(3), 336–343. https://doi.org/10.1111/medu.14380

Business Monitor International. 2018. *Kenya crime and security risk report*. Business Monitor International, https://search-proquest-com.libraryproxy.griffith.edu.au/docview/2046801073?pq-origsite=summon&https://search.proquest.com/central

Business World Disrupt. 2018. World Bank gives 750 Kenyan youth startup funding to stem unemployment crisis. *Business World*. http://bwdisrupt.businessworld.in/article/World-Bank-Gives-750-Kenyan-Youth-Startup-Funding-to-Stem-Unemployment-Crisis/10-02-2018-140271/

Camilleri, J. 2012. Human security: From theory to practice. In J. Camilleri & D. Atman (eds.), *Why Human Security Matters: Rethinking Australian Foreign Policy*. Allen & Unwin, Crows Nest, NSW, pp. 12–33.

Carey Jones, N.S. 1965. The decolonization of the White Highlands of Kenya. *The Geographical Journal*, *131*(2), 186–201. https://doi.org/10.2307/1793793

Carrier, N., & Kochore, H.H. 2014. Navigating ethnicity and electoral politics in northern Kenya: The case of the 2013 election. *Journal of Eastern African Studies*, *8*(1), 135–152. https://doi.org/10.1080/17531055.2013.871181

Česnulytė, E. 2015. 'I do not work: I do commercial sex work'. Ambiguities in the discourse and practice of selling sex in Mombasa, Kenya. *Development & Change*, *46*(5), 1159–1178. https://doi.org/10.1111/dech.12192

Charny, I.W. 2016. Worksheet for describing and categorizing a genocidal event: A new tool for assembling more objective data and classifying events of mass killing. *Social Sciences (Basel)*, *5*(3), 2. https://doi.org/10.3390/socsci5030031

Chege, M. 2008. Kenya: Back from the brink? *Journal of Democracy*, *19*(4), 125–139.

Chuma, J., & Okungu, V. 2011. Viewing the Kenyan health system through an equity lens: Implications for universal coverage. *International Journal for Equity in Health*, *10*(1), article 22, 1–14. https://doi.org/10.1186/1475-9276-10-22

CNN World. 2015. After Al-Shabaab's Garissa massacre, local Kenyan schools fear they're next. *CNN*. https://edition.cnn.com/2015/04/08/africa/kenya-shabaab-western-school/index.html

Connolly-Boutin, L., & Smit, B. 2015. Climate change, food security, and livelihoods in Sub-Saharan Africa. *Regional Environmental Change, 16*(2), 385–399. https://doi.org/10.1007/s10113-015-0761-x

Cooke, C. 2018. *Remembering the 1998 terrorist attack in Nairobi.* U.S Department of State. https://www.state.gov/remembering-the-1998-embassy-bombings-2/

Corno, L., Hildebrandt, N., & Voena, A. 2020. Age of marriage, weather shocks, and the direction of marriage payments. *Econometrica, 88*(3), 879–915. https://doi.org/10.3982/ECTA15505

Crea, T.M., & McFarland, M. 2015. Higher education for refugees: Lessons from a 4-year pilot project. *International Review of Education, 61*(2), 235–245. https://doi.org/10.1007/s11159-015-9484-y

Crilly, R. 2008. Briton shot dead in Kenyan robbery. *The Times.* https://www.thetimes.co.uk/article/briton-shot-dead-in-kenyan-robbery-zt99h30pt0m

Cumber, S.N., & Tsoka-Gwegweni, J. 2015. The health profile of street children in Africa: A literature review. *Journal of Public Health in Africa, 6*(2), 566. https://doi.org/10.4081/jphia.2015.566

Cussac, A. 2008. Muslims and politics in Kenya: The issue of the Kadhis' courts in the constitution review process. *Journal of Muslim Minority Affairs, 28*(2), 289–302. https://doi.org/10.1080/13602000802303227

D'Arcy, M., & Cornell, A. 2016. Devolution and corruption in Kenya: Everyone's turn to eat? *African Affairs, 115*(459), 246–273.

Dancer, H. 2017. An equal right to inherit? Women's land rights, customary law and constitutional reform in Tanzania. *Social & Legal Studies, 26*(3), 291–310. https://doi.org/10.1177/0964663916677560

Dávid-Barrett, E., Fazekas, M., Hellmann, O., Márk, L., & McCorley, C. 2020. Controlling corruption in development aid: New evidence from contract-level data. *Studies in Comparative International Development, 55*(4), 481–515.

Day, B. 2016. Australian aid after the 'Golden Consensus': From aid policy to development policy? *Australian Journal of International Affairs, 70*(6), 641–656.

De Zayas, A. 2014. Human rights and humanitarian law. *Nordic Journal of International Law, 61*(1–4), 259–261.

Deacon, G. 2012. Pentecostalism and development in Kibera informal settlement, Nairobi. *Development in Practice: Religion & Development, 22*(5–6), 663–674. https://doi.org/10.1080/09614524.2012.685874

Deb, T., & Giles, C. 2018. Kenya's empty nets: How cheap Chinese fish imports have hooked buyers. *The Philadelphia Tribune.* https://www.phillytrib.com/news/kenyas-empty-nets-how-cheap-chinese-fish-imports-have-hooked-buyers/article_7e36789c-5b05-58e5-9d21-a0d64bc3cca2.html

DeBoom, M.J. 2019. Who is afraid of 'debt-trap diplomacy'? Geopolitical narratives, agency and the multiscalar distribution of risk. *Area Development & Policy, 5*(1), 15–22. https://doi.org/10.1080/23792949.2019.1703556

Deghati, M. 2007. Nairobi's street children: Hope for Kenya's future generation. *The New Humanitarian.* https://www.irinnews.org/feature/2007/02/23/nairobi-s-street-children-hope-kenya-s-future-generation

Dembélé, M., & Oviawe, J. 2007. Introduction: Quality education in Africa: International commitments, local challenges and responses. *International Review of Education*, *53*(5–6), 473–483. https://doi.org/10.1007/s11159-007-9063-y

DFAT. 2014. *Aid program performance report 2012–13 Sub-Saharan Africa*. Australian Government Department of Foreign Affairs & Trade. https://www.dfat.gov.au/sites/default/files/africa-appr-2012-13.pdf

Dietrich, S. 2016. Donor political economies and the pursuit of aid effectiveness. *International Organization*, *70*(1), 65–102. https://doi.org/10.1017/S0020818315000302

Dodgson, J.E. 2017. About research: Qualitative methodologies. *Journal of Human Lactation*, *33*(2), 355–358. https://doi.org/10.1177/0890334417698693

Dolan, L.R. 2020. Rethinking foreign aid and legitimacy: Views from aid recipients in Kenya. *Studies in Comparative International Development*, *55*(2), 143–159. https://doi.org/10.1007/s12116-020-09302-9

Duffin, P., & Higgins, H. 2017. NSW teacher shot dead during Kenya robbery. *AAP Bulletin Wire*. https://search-proquest-com.libraryproxy.griffith.edu.au/docview/1952686347?pq-origsite=summon&https://search.proquest.com/central

Dwumfour, R.A., Agbloyor, E.K., & Abor, JY. 2017. Correlates of poverty in Africa: Exploring the roles of remittances, financial development, and natural resources. *International Journal of Social Economics*, *44*(12), 2033–2051. https://doi.org/10.1108/IJSE-12-2015-0319

Dyke, E., Edwards, N., McDowell, I., Muga, R., & Brown, S. 2014. Shaped by asymmetrical interdependence: A qualitative case study of the external influences on international non-governmental organizations' implementation of equity principles in HIV/AIDS work. *International Journal for Equity in Health*, *13*(1), 86. https://doi.org/10.1186/s12939-014-0086-2

EASF. 2021. *Overview*. East Africa Standby Force. https://www.easfcom.org/index.php/en/about-easf

Easterly, W. 2002. The cartel of good intentions: The problem of bureaucracy in foreign aid. *The Journal of Policy Reform*, *5*(4), 223–250. https://doi.org/10.1080/1384128032000096823

Easterly, W. 2003. Can foreign aid buy growth? *The Journal of Economic Perspectives*, *17*(3), 23–48.

Easterly, W. 2009. Can the West save Africa? *Journal of Economic Literature*, *47*(2), 373–447. https://doi.org/10.1257/jel.47.2.373

Easterly, W., & Williamson, C.R. 2011. Rhetoric *versus* reality: The best and worst of aid agency practices. *World Development*, *39*(11), 1930–1949. https://doi.org/10.1016/j.worlddev.2011.07.027

El-Khawas, M.A. 2005. Brain drain: Putting Africa between a rock and a hard place. *Mediterranean Quarterly*, *15*(4), 37–56.

Elu, J.U. 2013. NEA presidential address: Gender inequality and human development in Sub-Saharan Africa. *The Review of Black Political Economy*, *40*(2), 105–113. https://doi.org/10.1007/s12114-012-9152-4

Embleton, L., Ayuku, D., Makori, D., Kamanda, A., & Braitstein, P. 2018. Causes of death among street-connected children and youth in Eldoret, Kenya. *BMC*

International Health & Human Rights, *18*, article 19, 1–8. https://doi.org/10.1186/s12914-018-0160-8

Enns, C., & Bersaglio, B. 2020. On the coloniality of 'new' mega-infrastructure projects in East Africa. *Antipode*, *52*(1), 101–123. https://doi.org/10.1111/anti.12582

Ewing, T., & Aldhous, P. 1990. AIDS programme faces donor fatigue. *Nature*, *346*(6285), 595. https://doi.org/10.1038/346595a0

Falode, A.J. 2020. Small arms and light weapons (SALW) and transnational crime in Africa. *Vestnik Rossiĭskogo Universiteta Druzhby Narodov. Serii͡a Mezhdunarodnye otnoshenii͡a*, *20*(1), 158–169. https://doi.org/10.22363/2313-0660-2020-20-1-158-169

FAO. 2016. *Africa regional overview of food security and nutrition 2016*. Food & Agriculture Organization of the United Nations. http://www.fao.org/publications/rofsn-africa/en/

FAO. 2017. *Kenya and FAO partnering to build resilience and food and nutrition security*. Food & Agriculture Organization of the United Nations. http://www.fao.org/3/a-au195e.pdf

FAO. 2020. *About FAO*. Food & Agriculture Organization of the United Nations. http://www.fao.org/about/en/

Feikin, D.R., Nguyen, L.M., Adazu, K., Ombok, M., Audi, A., Slutsker, L., & Lindblade, K.A. 2009. The impact of distance of residence from a peripheral health facility on pediatric health utilisation in rural western Kenya. *Tropical Medicine & International Health*, *14*(1), 54–61. https://doi.org/10.1111/j.1365-3156.2008.02193.x

Fenske, J. 2015. African polygamy: Past and present. *Journal of Development Economics*, *117*, 58–73. https://doi.org/10.1016/j.jdeveco.2015.06.005

Florence, N. 2013. Bukusu (Kenya) folktales: How women perpetuate patriarchy. *International Feminist Journal of Politics*, *15*(3), 370–390. https://doi.org/10.1080/14616742.2012.744175

Foreign Aid Assistance. 2017. *Kenya Foreign Assistance*. Foreign Assistance. http://www.foreignassistance.gov/explore/country/Kenya

Forsyth, M. 2016. The regulation of witchcraft and sorcery practices and beliefs. *Annual Review of Law & Social Science*, *12*(1), 331–351. https://doi.org/10.1146/annurev-lawsocsci-110615-084600

Foster, T., McSorley, B., & Willetts, J. 2019. Comparative performance evaluation of handpump water-supply technologies in northern Kenya and the Gambia. *Hydrogeology Journal*, *27*(2), 535–551. https://doi.org/10.1007/s10040-018-1865-4

Frankema, E.H.P. 2012. The origins of formal education in Sub-Saharan Africa: Was British rule more benign? *European Review of Economic History*, *16*(4), 335–355. https://doi.org/10.1093/ereh/hes009

Friedman, W. 2018. Corruption and averting AIDS deaths. *World Development*, *110*, 13–25.

Friedman, W., Kremer, M., Miguel, E., & Thornton, R. 2016. Education as liberation? *Economica*, *83*(329), 1–30. https://doi.org/10.1111/ecca.12168

Fuo, O.N. 2015. Public participation in decentralised governments in Africa: Making ambitious constitutional guarantees more responsive. *African Human Rights Law Journal*, *15*(1), 167–191.

Gearhart, R. & Abdulrehman, M.S. 2014. Concepts of illness among the Swahili of Lamu, Kenya. *Journal of Transcultural Nursing*, *25*(3), 218–222. https://doi.org/10.1177/1043659613515713

Gelot, L. 2020. Deradicalization as soft counter-insurgency: Distorted interactions between Somali traditional authorities and intervening organizations. *Journal of Intervention & Statebuilding: Security Governance/IOs in Africa*, *14*(2), 253–270. https://doi.org/10.1080/17502977.2020.1734390

Gershman, B. 2016. Witchcraft beliefs and the erosion of social capital: Evidence from Sub-Saharan Africa and beyond. *Journal of Development Economics*, *120*, 182–208. https://doi.org/10.1016/j.jdeveco.2015.11.005

Glanville, L. 2010. The international community's responsibility to protect. *Global Responsibility to Protect*, *2*(3), 287–306. https://doi.org/10.1163/187598410X500408

Glewwe, P., Kremer, M., & Moulin, S. 2009. Many children left behind? Textbooks and test scores in Kenya. *American Economic Journal: Applied Economics*, *1*(1), 112–135. https://doi.org/10.1257/app.1.1.112

Gopal, S., Ma, Y., Xin, C., Pitts, J., & Were, L. 2019. Characterizing the spatial determinants and prevention of malaria in Kenya. *International Journal of Environmental Research & Public Health*, *16*(24). https://doi.org/10.3390/ijerph16245078

Grépin, K.A. 2009. Efficiency considerations of donor fatigue, universal access to ARTs and health systems. *Sexually Transmitted Infections*, *88*(2), 75–78. https://doi.org/10.1136/sextrans-2011-050148

Gueye, M. 2018. Colonialism in Africa: A revisionist perspective. *The Journal of Pan African Studies*, *12*(1), 111–122.

Gulrajani, N., & Swiss, L. 2019. Donor proliferation to what ends? New donor countries and the search for legitimacy. *Canadian Journal of Development Studies/Revue Canadienne d'Études Du Développement*, *40*(3), 348–368. https://doi.org/10.1080/02255189.2019.1543652

Hajir, A. 2017. Four killed in IED attack in Garissa. *The Daily Nation*. https://nation.africa/kenya/news/four-killed-in-ied-attack-in-garissa-406948

Hale, F. 2015. Nils Astrup and indigenous African cultures: A study in evolving missionary attitudes. *Journal for the Study of Religion*, *28*(2), 42–63.

Halpern, C.L. 2011. Ministry of fear. *The New York Times*. https://www.nytimes.com/2011/10/30/magazine/at-an-african-convent-desperate-knocks-and-hours.html

Hansen, T.O., & Sriram, C.L. 2015. Fighting for justice (and survival): Kenyan civil society accountability strategies and their enemies. *The International Journal of Transitional Justice*, *9*(3), 407–427. https://doi.org/10.1093/ijtj/ijv012

Harrington, L.J., & Manji, A. 2013. Satire and the politics of corruption in Kenya. *Social & Legal Studies*, *22*(1), 3–23. https://doi.org/10.1177/0964663912458113

Harrington, L.J., & Otto, F.E.L. 2020. Reconciling theory with the reality of African heatwaves. *Nature Climate Change*, *10*(9), 796–798. https://doi.org/10.1038/s41558-020-0851-8

Harris, J. 2014. Transnational capitalism and class formation. *Science & Society*, *78*(3), 312–333. https://doi.org/10.1521/siso.2014.78.3.312

Harris, J. 2015. Transnational capital and the technology of domination and desire. *Race & Class*, *57*(1), 3–19. https://doi.org/10.1177/0306396815581780

Harris, J. 2018. China's road from socialism to global capitalism. *Third World Quarterly*, *39*(9), 1711–1726. https://doi.org/10.1080/01436597.2018.1496791

Hassan, M., & O'Mealia, T. 2018. Uneven accountability in the wake of political violence: Evidence from Kenya's ashes and archives. *Journal of Peace Research*, *55*(2), 161–174. https://doi.org/10.1177/0022343317751836

Hathaway, O.A., Crootof, R., Hessel, D., Shu, J., & Weiner, S. 2016. Consent is not enough: Why states must respect the intensity threshold in transnational conflict. *University of Pennsylvania Law Review*, *165*(1), 1–47.

Hershey, M. 2013. Explaining the non-governmental organization (NGO) boom: The case of HIV/AIDS NGOs in Kenya. *Journal of Eastern African Studies*, *7*(4), 671–690. https://doi.org/10.1080/17531055.2013.818776

Hibbard, S.D. 2015. Clientelism and corruption in Kenya. *ProQuest LLC*. https://search.proquest.com/openview/125853b4574766628ffea2d36659ceb5/1?pq-origsite=gscholar&cbl=18750&diss=y

Hill Jr., D.W. 2016. Avoiding obligation: Reservations to human rights treaties. *Journal of Conflict Resolution*, *60*(6), 1129–1158. https://doi.org/10.1177/0022002714567947

Hooghe, M., Vanhoutte, B., Hardyns, W., & Bircan, T. 2010. Unemployment, inequality, poverty and crime: Spatial distribution patterns of criminal acts in Belgium, 2001–06. *The British Journal of Criminology*, *51*(1), 1–20. https://doi.org/10.1093/bjc/azq067

Hrubec, M., & Uhde, Z. 2018. Global conflicts and local interactions: Contradictions of global capitalism and civil society. *Critical Sociology*, *45*(6), 777–783. https://doi.org/10.1177/0896920518798880

Huband, M. 1992. Kenyan elections may reopen old tribal wounds. *Mark Huband*. http://www.markhuband.com/kenyan-elections-may-reopen-old-tribal-wounds/

Hübschle, A. 2011. From theory to practice: Exploring the organised crime-terror nexus in Sub-Saharan Africa. *Perspectives on Terrorism*, *5*(3–4), 81–95.

Hughes, L. 2008. Mining the Maasai reserve: The story of Magadi. *Journal of Eastern African Studies*, *2*(1), 134–164. https://doi.org/10.1080/17531050701847326

Hughes, R.C. 2013. 'Science in the hands of love': British evangelical missionaries and colonial development in Africa, c. 1940–60. *The Journal of Imperial & Commonwealth History*, *41*(5), 823–842. https://doi.org/10.1080/03086534.2013.814255

Hurd, I. 2011. *International Organizations: Politics, Law, Practice*. Cambridge University Press, New York.

Hurst, E. 2017. Local villages and global networks: The language and migration experiences of African skilled migrant academics. *Globalisation, Societies and Education*, *15*(1), 50–67.

Ibrahim, S.S., Ibrahim, A., Allah, A.N., & Saulawa, L.A. 2016. Building of a community cattle ranch and radio frequency identification (RFID) technology as alternative methods of curtailing cattle rustling in Katsina State. *Pastoralism: Research, Policy & Practice*, *6*(1), 1–9. https://doi.org/10.1186/s13570-016-0055-z

Idejiora-Kalu, N. 2019. Understanding the effects of the resolutions of the 1884–85 Berlin conference to Africa's development and Euro-Africa relations. *Prague Papers on the History of International Relations*, *2*, 99–108.

Ilie, S., & Rose, P. 2016. Is equal access to higher education in South Asia and Sub-Saharan Africa achievable by 2030? *Higher Education*, *72*(4), 435–455.

Inderfurth, K.F., Fabrycky, D., & Cohen, S.P. 2005. Save Pakistan from 'donor fatigue'. *Brookings*. https://www.brookings.edu/opinions/save-pakistan-from-donor-fatigue/

Indo Asian News Service. 2018. DAI's global services center to come up in Hyderabad. *Outlook: The News Scroll*. https://www.outlookindia.com/newsscroll/dais-global-services-center-to-come-up-in-hyderabad/1421593

Inglehart, R.F., & Norris, P. 2012. The four horsemen of the apocalypse: Understanding human security. *Scandinavian Political Studies*, *35*(1), 71–96. https://doi.org/10.1111/j.1467-9477.2011.00281.x

Isaac, O. 2019. Transport infrastructure development in Kenya: How connectivity impacts eastern Africa regional integration. *Insight on Africa*, *11*(2), 200–218. https://doi.org/10.1177/0975087819845205

Islam, F. 2019. Aid budget to be used by international trade department. *BBC*. https://www.bbc.com/news/business-49068882

Islam, M.R. 2014. Improving development ownership among vulnerable people: Challenges of NGOs' community empowerment projects in Bangladesh. *Asian Social Work & Policy Review*, *8*(3), 193–209. https://doi.org/10.1111/aswp.12035

Jablonski, R.S. 2014. How aid targets votes: The impact of electoral incentives on foreign aid distribution. *World Politics*, *66*(2), 293–330. https://doi.org/10.1017/S0043887114000045

Jett, D. 2016. What can peacekeepers do if there is no peace to keep? *Middle East Policy*, *23*(4), 149–158. https://doi.org/10.1111/mepo.12240

Jewitt, S., & Ryley, H. 2014. It's a girl thing: Menstruation, school attendance, spatial mobility and wider gender inequalities in Kenya. *Geoforum*, *56*, 137–147. https://doi.org/10.1016/j.geoforum.2014.07.006

Joseph, O. 2009. Horror of Kenya's 'witch' iynchings. *BBC*. http://news.bbc.co.uk/2/hi/africa/8119201.stm

Jowell, M. 2017. The unintended consequences of foreign military assistance in Africa: An analysis of peacekeeping training in Kenya. *Journal of Eastern African Studies*, *12*(1), 102–119. https://doi.org/10.1080/17531055.2017.1418187

Juma, K., Juma, P.A., Mohamed, S.F., Owuor, J., Wanyoike, A., Mulabi, D., Odinya, G., Njeru, M., & Yonga, G. 2019. First Africa non-communicable disease research conference 2017: Sharing evidence and identifying research priorities. *Journal of Global Health*, *8*(2), 1–14. https://doi.org/10.7189/jogh.09.010201

Kabranian-Melkonian, S. 2015. Ethical concerns with refugee research. *Journal of Human Behaviour in the Social Environment*, *25*(7), 714–722.

Kagwanja, P.M. 2003. Facing Mount Kenya or facing Mecca? The Mungiki, ethnic violence and the politics of the Moi succession in Kenya, 1987–2002. *African Affairs*, *102*(406), 25–49. https://doi.org/10.1093/oxfordjournals.afraf.a138810

Kaime-Atterhög, W., Persson, L., & Ahlberg, B.M. 2017. 'With an open heart we receive the children': Caregivers' strategies for reaching and caring for street children in Kenya. *Journal of Social Work*, *17*(5), 579–598. https://doi.org/10.1177/1468017316651989

Kanyinga, K. 2009. The legacy of the white highlands: Land rights, ethnicity and the post-2007 election violence in Kenya. *Journal of Contemporary African Studies*, *27*(3), 325–344. https://doi.org/10.1080/02589000903154834

Karanja, S., & Kilonzo, E. 2015. NGOs received Sh6b funds from unknown sources – report. *Daily Nation*. https://nation.africa/kenya/news/ngos-received-sh6b-funds-from-unknown-sources-report-1128018

Kasbaoui, T., & Nechad, A. 2018. Spectrum of aid and the illusion of a Marshall Plan for Africa. In M. Przygoda, L. Lovrencic Butkovic, & E. Szymanska (eds.), *Economic and Social Development: Book of Proceedings*. Varazdin: Varazdin Development & Entrepreneurship Agency (VADEA), pp. 133–144.

Kassie, M., Ndiritu, S.W., & Stage, J. 2014. What determines gender inequality in household food security in Kenya? Application of exogenous switching treatment regression. *World Development*, *56*, 153–171. https://doi.org/10.1016/j.worlddev.2013.10.025

Keller, J., Mboya, B.O., Sinclair, J., Githua, O.W., Mulinge, M., Bergholz, L., Paiva, L., Golden, N., & Kapphahn, C. 2017. A 6-week school curriculum improves boys' attitudes and behaviors related to gender-based violence in Kenya. *Journal of Interpersonal Violence*, *32*(4), 535–557. https://doi.org/10.1177/0886260515586367

Kelly, K. 2017. A different type of lighting research—A qualitative methodology. *Lighting Research & Technology*, *49*(8), 933–942. https://doi.org/10.1177/1477153516659901

Kimari, W. 2018. Activists, care work, and the 'cry of the ghetto' in Nairobi, Kenya. *Humanities & Social Sciences Communications*, *4*(1), 1–7. https://doi.org/10.1057/s41599-018-0078-8

Kimemia, D. 2013. *Organizational culture and corruption: A multiple case study of non-governmental organizations in Kenya*. Scholars Compass. https://scholarscompass.vcu.edu/cgi/viewcontent.cgi?article=3960&context=etd

King, E. 2018. What Kenyan youth want and why it matters for peace. *African Studies Review*, *61*(1), 134–157. https://doi.org/10.1017/asr.2017.98

King, K. 2010. China's cooperation in education and training with Kenya: A different model? *International Journal of Educational Development*, *30*(5), 488–496. https://doi.org/10.1016/j.ijedudev.2010.03.014

Kingery, F.P., Naanyu, V., Allen, W., & Patel, P. 2016. Photovoice in Kenya: Using a community-based participatory research method to identify health needs. *Qualitative Health Research*, *26*(1), 92–104. https://doi.org/10.1177/1049732315617738

King-Okumu, C., Jillo, B., Kinyanjui, J., & Jarso, I. 2018. Devolving water governance in the Kenyan Arid Lands: From top-down drought and flood emergency response to locally driven water resource development planning. *International*

Journal of Water Resources Development, *34*(4), 675–697. https://doi.org/10.1080/07900627.2017.1357539

Kisirkoi, F.K., & Mse, G.S. 2016. Education access and retention for street children: Perspectives from Kenya. *Journal of Education & Practice*, *7*(2), 88–94.

Kitaoka, S. 2016. Sustainable development goals and Japan's official development assistance policy: Human security, national interest, and a more proactive contribution to peace. *Asia-Pacific Review*, *23*(1), 32–41.

Kiura, A.W. 2014. Constrained agency on contraceptive use among Somali refugee women in the Kakuma refugee camp in Kenya. *Gender, Technology & Development*, *18*(1), 147–161. https://doi.org/10.1177/0971852413515321

Klaus, K. 2017. Contentious land narratives and the nonescalation of election violence: Evidence from Kenya's coast region. *African Studies Review*, *60*(2), 51–72. https://doi.org/10.1017/asr.2017.2

Krennerich, M. 2014. Social security—Just as much a human right in developing countries and emerging markets. *Verfassung Und Recht in Übersee*, *47*(1), 105–123. https://doi.org/10.5771/0506-7286-2014-1-105

Kristjanson, P., Mango, N., Krishna, A., Radeny, M., & Johnson, N. 2010. Understanding poverty dynamics in Kenya. *Journal of International Development*, *22*(7), 978–996. https://doi.org/10.1002/jid.1598

Kuada, J. 2013. Infrastructure and development in Africa. *African Journal of Economic & Management Studies*, *4*(1). https://doi.org/10.1108/ajems.2013.43904aaa.001

Kukrety, N., & Mohanty, S. 2011. Putting gender equality at the heart of social protection: Lessons from Oxfam GB's experience with safety net programming. *Gender & Development: Social Protection*, *19*(2), 271–281. https://doi.org/10.1080/13552074.2011.592638

Langan, M. 2015. Budget support and Africa–European union relations: Free market reform and neo-colonialism? *European Journal of International Relations*, *21*(1), 101–121. https://doi.org/10.1177/1354066113516813

Lau, C., Gachugu, E., Johnson, E., & Marks, L. 2018. Using SMS technology to survey low-income youth: Lessons from a vocational education tracking study in Kenya. *Journal of International Development*, *30*(6), 1060–1063. https://doi.org/10.1002/jid.3373

Lawley, J. 2015. Achievements of the British colonial service: A retrospective view. *The Commonwealth Journal of International Affairs*, *104*(3), 267–280. https://doi.org/10.1080/00358533.2015.1053710

Leman, P. 2011. African oral law and the critique of colonial modernity in *The Trial of Jomo Kenyatta*. *Law & Literature*, *23*(1), 26–47.

Lesorogol, C.K. 2008. Setting themselves apart: Education, capabilities, and sexuality among Samburu women in Kenya. *Anthropological Quarterly*, *81*(3), 551–577. https://doi.org/10.1353/anq.0.0020

Longobardo, M. 2015. Genocide, obligations erga omnes, and the responsibility to protect: Remarks on a complex convergence. *The International Journal of Human Rights*, *19*(8), 1199–1212. https://doi.org/10.1080/13642987.2015.1082834

Machangu, H.M. 2015. Vulnerability of elderly women to witchcraft accusations among the Fipa of Sumbawanga, 1961–2010. *Journal of International Women's Studies*, *16*(2), 274–284.

MacLean, L.M., Brass, J.N., Carley, S., El-Arini, A., & Breen, S. 2015. Democracy and the distribution of NGOs promoting renewable energy in Africa. *The Journal of Development Studies*, *51*(6), 725–742. https://doi.org/10.1080/00220388.2014.989994

Maekawa, I. 2015. Neo-colonialism reconsidered: A case study of East Africa in the 1960s and 1970s. *The Journal of Imperial & Commonwealth History*, *43*(2), 317–341. https://doi.org/10.1080/03086534.2014.982406

Maiyo, J. 2015. Education and poverty correlates: A case of Trans-Nzoia County, Kenya. *International Journal of Educational Administration & Policy Studies*, *7*(7), 142–143.

Maluwa, T., & Katz, A. 2020. Who is a refugee?: Twenty-five years of domestic implementation and judicial interpretation of the 1969 OAW and 1951 UN refugee conventions in post-apartheid South Africa. *Indiana Journal of Global Legal Studies*, *27*(2), 129–205. https://doi.org/10.2979/indjglolegstu.27.2.0129

Mani, A., Mullainathan, S., Shafir, E., & Zhao, J. 2013. Poverty impedes cognitive function. *Science*, *341*(6149), 976–980. https://doi.org/10.1126/science.1238041

Marita, E., Oule, J., Mungai, M., Thiam, S., & Ilako, F. 2016. Capacity and readiness of civil society organisations to implement community case management of malaria in Kenya. *The Pan African Medical Journal*, *25*(Suppl 2), 2, 6. https://doi.org/10.11604/pamj.supp.2016.25.2.9305

Markham, J. 2008. Kenya and foreign aid. *The Globe & Mail*. https://www.theglobeandmail.com/opinion/letters/kenya-and-foreign-aid/article667185/

Martinez, G.M. 2016. *Unraveling red tape: Foreign aid allocation and the domestic bureaucracy*. IDEALS. https://www.ideals.illinois.edu/handle/2142/90703

Masuku, D. 2013. Australian man Patrick John Richer shot dead during robbery in Kenya. *ABC News*. https://www.abc.net.au/news/2013-11-18/australian-shot-dead-during-robbery-in-kenya/5098046

Matasci, D., Jerónimo, M.B., & Dores, H.G. 2020. *Education and Development in Colonial and Postcolonial Africa: Policies, Paradigms, and Entanglements, 1890s–1980s*. Cham: Springer International Publishing, Kindle Edition.

Matthews, S. 2017. The role of NGOs in Africa: Are they a force for good? *The Conversation*. https://theconversation.com/the-role-of-ngos-in-africa-are-they-a-force-for-good-76227

Mawdsley, E. 2010. Non-DAC donors and the changing landscape of foreign aid: The (in)significance of India's development cooperation with Kenya. *Journal of Eastern African Studies*, *4*(2), 361–379. https://doi.org/10.1080/17531055.2010.487345

McCormick, D., & Schmitz, H. 2011. Donor proliferation and co-ordination: Experience of Kenya and Indonesia. *Journal of Asian and African Studies*, *46*(2), 149–168.

McNamara, K.R. 2019. Constitutionalization above the state: How after victory broke anarchy. *The British Journal of Politics & International Relations*, *21*(1), 40–46. https://doi.org/10.1177/1369148118791400

Meel, B.L. 2003. 1. The myth of child rape as a cure for HIV/AIDS in Transkei: A case report. *Medicine, Science, & the Law*, *43*(1), 85–88. https://doi.org/10.1258/rsmmsl.43.1.85

Meier Zu Selhausen, F., & Weisdorf, J. 2016. A colonial legacy of African gender inequality? Evidence from Christian kampala, 1895–2011. *The Economic History Review*, *69*(1), 229–257.

Mercer, C. 2016. NGOs, civil society and democratization: A critical review of the literature. *Progress in Development Studies*, *2*(1), 5–22. https://doi.org/10.1191/1464993402ps027ra

Mikulak, M. 2003. Street children in Kenya: Voices of children in search of a childhood. Philip Kilbride, Collette Suda, Enos Njeru. *Journal of Anthropological Research*, *59*(3), 390–392 https://doi.org/10.1086/jar5933631511

Mills, J.E., & Birks, M. 2014. *Qualitative Methodology: A Practical Guide*. London: Sage Publishing.

Ministry of Health. 2020. *Covid-19*. https://www.health.go.ke/covid-19/

Mkutu, K.A., & Sabala, K. 2007. Private security companies in Kenya and dilemmas for security. *Journal of Contemporary African Studies*, *25*(3), 391–416. https://doi.org/10.1080/02589000701662442

Moe, L.W., & Geis, A. 2020. From liberal interventionism to stabilisation: A new consensus on norm-downsizing in interventions in Africa. *Global Constitutionalism*, *9*(2), 387–412. https://doi.org/10.1017/S204538171900039X

Mofokeng, T. 1988. Black Christians, the Bible and liberation. *Journal of Black Theology in South Africa*, *2*(1) 34–42.

Mogire, E. 2009. Refugee realities: Refugee rights versus state security in Kenya and Tanzania. *Transformation*, *26*(1), 15–29. 10.1177/0265378809102173

Monbiot, G. 2016. Neoliberalism – The ideology at the root of all our problems. *The Guardian*. https://www.theguardian.com/books/2016/apr/15/neoliberalism-ideology-problem-george-monbiot

Mooney, G. 2009. Review of Dead aid: Why aid is not working and how there is another way for Africa. Australian and New Zealand Journal of Public Health, *33*(4), 397–398. https://doi.org/10.1111/j1753-6405200900416x

Morgan, W.T.W. 1963. The 'White Highlands' of Kenya. *The Geographical Journal*, *129*(2), 140–155.

Morumbasi, S.K., & Amuhaya, C. 2016. A networks analysis of terrorism in Africa: Implications for Kenya. *Vestnik Rossiĭskogo Universiteta Druzhby Narodov Serii͡a Mezhdunarodnye otnosheni͡a*, *16*(2), 265–273.

Moyer, J.M., Sinclair, A.J., & Spaling, H. 2012. Working for God and sustainability: The activities of faith-based organizations in Kenya. *VOLUNTAS*, *23*(4), 959–992. https://doi.org/10.1007/s11266-011-9245-x

Moyo, D. 2017. *Dead Aid: Why Aid is Not Working and Now There is a Better Way for Africa*. New York: Farrar, Straus and Giroux.

Mpyangu, C.M., & Bukuluki, P. 2018. The African conception of sacrifice and its relationship with child sacrifice. *International Letters of Social & Humanistic Sciences*, *41*, 12–24.

Mshana, G., Plummer, M.L., Wamoyi, J., Shigongo, Z.S., Ross, D.A., & Wight, D. 2006. 'She was bewitched and caught an illness similar to AIDS': AIDS and sexually transmitted infection causation beliefs in rural northern Tanzania. *Culture, Health & Sexuality*, *8*(1), 45–58. https://doi.org/10.1080/13691050500469731

Mugambi, F.N., & Mbuba, J.M. 2011. Approaches to crime control and order maintenance in transitional societies: The role of village headmen, chiefs, sub-chiefs and administration police in rural Kenya. *African Journal of Criminology & Justice Studies*, *4*(2), 1–12.

Muhammad, A., D'Souza, A., & Amponsah, W. 2013. Violence, instability, and trade: Evidence from Kenya's cut flower sector. *World Development*, *51*, 20–31. https://doi.org/10.1016/j.worlddev.2013.05.004

Muisyo, V., & Ibrahim, M. 2018. Somalia's traditional textiles fray at the seams as cheap imports flood markets. *African News*. https://www.africanews.com/2018/05/26/somalia-s-traditional-textiles-fray-at-the-seams-as-cheap-imports-flood-markets/

Musangi, P. 2017. Women land property rights in Kenya. *Land Portal*. https://landportal.org/node/52225#:~:text=Customary%20practices%20in%20Kenya%20generally,Kenyan%20women%20equal%20inheritance%20rights

Mwangi, E. 2010. The incomplete rebellion: Mau Mau movement in twenty-first-century Kenyan popular culture. *Africa Today*, *57*(2), 87–113.

Mwaniki, C. 2022. Kenyan's average monthly income climbs to sh20,123. *Business Daily*. https://www.businessdailyafrica.com/bd/economy/kenyans-average-income-of-sh20-123-hits-six-year-high--4043204

Mwaura, N. 2005. *Kenya Today: Breaking the Yoke of Colonialism in Africa*. New York: Algora Publishing.

Ngendakurio, J.B. 2017. Congolese men and women of good hope: The legacies of refugee camps for work market readiness in hyper-diverse cities. Master's thesis, Griffith University. https://doi.org/10.25904/1912/2758

Nicoll, A., & Delaney, J. 2010. AU's regional force still on standby. *Strategic Comments*, *16*(10), 1–3. https://doi.org/101080/13567882010549775

Nikulkov, A., Barrett, C.B., Mude, A.G., & Wein, L.M. 2016. Assessing the impact of US food assistance delivery policies on child mortality in northern Kenya. *PLoS One*, *11*(12), e0168432. https://doi.org/10.1371/journal.pone.0168432

Njoh, A.J., & Ananga, E. 2016. Erratum to: The development hypothesis of women empowerment in the millennium development goals tested in the context of women's access to land in Africa. *Social Indicators Research*, *128*(2), 89–104. https://doi.org/10.1007/s11205-015-1047-x

Njororai, W.W.S. 2009. Colonial legacy, minorities and association football in Kenya. *Soccer & Society*, *10*(6), 866–882.

Njoya, E.T., & Seetaram, N. 2018. Tourism contribution to poverty alleviation in Kenya: A dynamic computable general equilibrium analysis. *Journal of Travel Research*, *57*(4), 513–524. https://doi.org/10.1177/0047287517700317

Njuguna, J., Mwangi, P., & Kamau, N. 2014. Incentives among health workers in a remote Kenyan district: Implications for proposed county health system. *Journal of Health Care for the Poor & Underserved*, *25*(1), 204–214. https://doi.org/10.1353/hpu.2014.0029

Njuki, R., Okal, J., Warren, C.E., Obare, F., Abuya, T., Kanya, L., Undie, C., Bellows, B., & Askew, I. 2012. Exploring the effectiveness of the output-based aid voucher program to increase uptake of gender-based violence recovery services in Kenya: A qualitative evaluation. *BMC Public Health*, *12*(1), 426. https://doi.org/10.1186/1471-2458-12-426

Nkonge, D.K. 2014. The church missionary society's burden: Theological education for a self-supporting, self-governing, and self-propagating African Anglican church in Kenya 1844–1930. *Anglican & Episcopal History*, *83*(1), 20–41.

Nour, N.M. 2006. Health consequences of child marriage in Africa. *Emerging Infectious Diseases*, *12*(11), 1644–1649. https://doi.org/10.3201/eid1211.060510

Ntarangwi, M. 2003. The challenges of education and development in post-colonial Kenya. *Africa Development*, 28(3–4), 211–228.

Nyambedha, E.O., & Aagaard-Hansen, J. 2010. Educational consequences of orphanhood and poverty in western Kenya. *Educational Studies*, *36*(5), 555–567. https://doi.org/10.1080/03055691003728981

Obala, L.M., & Mattingly, M. 2014. Ethnicity, corruption and violence in urban land conflict in Kenya. *Urban Studies*, *51*(13), 2735–2751. https://doi.org/10.1177/0042098013513650

Obeng-Odoom, F. 2015. Africa: On the rise, but to where? *The Forum for Social Economics*, *44*(3), 234–250.

Obeng-Odoom, F. 2020. Why inequality persists in Africa. *Review of African Political Economy*, *47*(163), 135–143.

Obiora, O.L., Maree, J.E., & Nkosi-Mafutha, N. 2020. Female genital mutilation in Africa: Scoping the landscape of evidence. *International Journal of Africa Nursing Sciences*, *12*(100189), 1–12. https://doi.org/10.1016/j.ijans.2019.100189

Ochieng, J., Kirimi, L., & Makau, J. 2016. Adapting to climate variability and change in rural Kenya: Farmer perceptions, strategies and climate trends. *Natural Resources Forum*, *41*(4), 195–208. https://doi.org/10.1111/1477-894712111

Odero, M., Hatcher, A.M., Bryant, C., Onono, M., Romito, P., Bukusi, E.A., & Turan, J.M. 2014. Responses to and resources for intimate partner violence: Qualitative findings from women, men, and service providers in rural Kenya. *Journal of Interpersonal Violence*, *29*(5), 783–805. https://doi.org/10.1177/0886260513505706

OECD. 2020. *Official Development Assistance (ODA)*. https://www.oecd.org/dac/financing-sustainable-development/development-finance-standards/official-development-assistance.htm

Öhman, A. 2005. Qualitative methodology for rehabilitation research. *Journal of Rehabilitation Medicine*, *37*(5), 273–280. https://doi.org/10.1080/16501970510040056

Olu, O., Petu, A., Ovberedjo, M., & Muhongerwa, D. 2017. South-south cooperation as a mechanism to strengthen public health services in Africa: Experiences, challenges and a call for concerted action. *The Pan African Medical Journal*, *28*, 40. https://doi.org/10.11604/pamj.2017.28.40.12201

Oluoko-Odingo, A.A. 2011. Vulnerability and adaptation to food insecurity and poverty in Kenya. *Annals of the Association of American Geographers*, *101*(1), 1–20. https://doi.org/10.1080/00045608.2010.532739

Ongong'a, J.J., & Akaranga, S,I. 2014. The suppression of women by religion: A Kenyan example. *Journal of Educational Policy & Entrepreneurial Research (JEPER)*, *1*(4), 48–60.

Oxfam. 2017. *Kenya.* Oxfam. https://www.oxfam.org/en/countries/kenya

Parsons, T.H. 2017. Mau Mau's army of clerks: Colonial military service and the Kenya land freedom army in Kenya's national imagination. *Journal of African History*, *58*(2), 285–309. https://doi.org/10.1017/S0021853717000044.

Peterman, A., Neijhoft, A.N., Cook, S., & Palermo, T.M. 2017. Understanding the linkages between social safety nets and childhood violence: A review of the evidence from low- and middle-income countries. *Health Policy & Planning*, *32*(7), 1049–1071. https://doi.org/10.1093/heapol/czx033

Plummer, A. 2019. Kenya and China's labour relations: Infrastructural development for whom, by whom? *Africa*, *89*(4), 680–695. https://doi.org/10.1017/S0001972019000858

Polkovnikova-Wamoto, A., Mathai, M., Vander Stoep, A., & Kumar, M. 2016. 'Haven of safety' and 'secure base': A qualitative inquiry into factors affecting child attachment security in Nairobi, Kenya. *Vulnerable Children & Youth Studies*, *11*(4), 286–296. https://doi.org/101080/17450128.2016.1201237

Pollack, D. 2011. International legal note: Salaries of CEOs of international NGOs: Ensuring fair compensation while avoiding populist rage. *International Social Work*, *54*(4), 599–604. https://doi.org/10.1177/0020872811403517

Pratt, C. 1999. Competing rationales for Canadian development assistance: Reducing global poverty, enhancing Canadian prosperity and security, or advancing global human security. *International Journal (Toronto)*, *54*(2), 306–323.

Puri, J., Aladysheva, A., Iversen, V., Ghorpade, Y., & Brück, T. 2017. Can rigorous impact evaluations improve humanitarian assistance? *Journal of Development Effectiveness*, *9*(4), 519–542. https://doi.org/101080/19439342.2017.1388267

Quazi, R.M., Ballentine, W.E., Bindu, F., & Blyden, L. 2019. Multilateral foreign aid, bilateral foreign aid, and foreign direct investment in Latin America. *International Journal of Economics & Financial Issues*, *9*(2), 284–290.

Rajput, A. 2019. Governance: Keeping NGOs in check. *gfiles*. https://www.gfilesindia.com/governance-keeping-ngos-in-check/

Rasmussen, J. (2010). Mungiki as youth movement: Revolution, gender and generational politics in Nairobi, Kenya. *YOUNG*, *18*(3), 301–319. https://doi.org/10.1177/110330881001800304

Ray, S. 2018. Beyond divide and rule: Explaining the link between British colonialism and ethnic violence. *Nationalism & Ethnic Politics*, *24*(4), 367–388. 10.1080/13537113.2018.1522745

Reese, G., Berthold, A., & Steffens, M.C. 2012. We are the world—And they are not: Prototypicality for the world community, legitimacy, and responses to global inequality. *Political Psychology*, *33*(5), 683–700. https://doi.org/10.1111/j1467-9221201200892x

Robinson, W.I. 2014. *Global Capitalism and the Crisis of Humanity*. New York: Cambridge University Press, p. 1.

Robinson, W.I., & Harris, J. 2000. Towards a global ruling class? Globalization and the transnational capitalist class. *Science & Society*, *64*(1), 11–54.

Roche, R., Bain, R., & Cumming, O. 2017. A long way to go—Estimates of combined water, sanitation and hygiene coverage for 25 Sub-Saharan African countries. *PLoS One*, *12*(2), article e0171783. https://doi.org/10.1371/journal.pone.0171783

Rončević, N., Stojadinović, A., & Batrnekantonić, D. 2013. Street children. *Srpski Arhiv Za Celokupno Lekarstvo*, *141*(11–12), 835–841.

Rutten, M., & Owuor, S. 2009. Weapons of mass destruction: Land, ethnicity and the 2007 elections in Kenya. *Journal of Contemporary African Studies*, *27*(3), 305–324. https://doi.org/10.1080/02589000903118904

Saaid Ali, Abd Elrhman Elzahi. 2017. The challenges facing poverty alleviation and financial inclusion in North-East Kenya Province (NEKP). *International Journal of Social Economics*, *44*(12), 2208–2223. https://doi.org/10.1108/IJSE-05-2016-0133

Sachs, J. 2014. *The Case for Aid.* Foreign Policy. https://foreignpolicy.com/2014/01/21/the-case-for-aid/

Saeteurn, M.C. 2017. 'A beacon of hope for the community': The role of chavakali secondary school in late colonial and early independent Kenya. *Journal of African History*, *58*(2), 311–329. https://doi.org/10.1017/S0021853716000682

Sales, L. 2015. Peter Dutton rejects international criticism at UN over treatment of asylum seekers. *ABC.* https://www.abc.net.au/7.30/peter-dutton-rejects-international-criticism-at-un/6929188

Schnabel, L. 2016. Religion and gender equality worldwide: A country-level analysis. *Social Indicators Research*, *129*(2), 893–907. https://doi.org/10.1007/s11205-015-1147-7

Schulman, S., & Williams, P.D. 2012. Photo essay: AMISOM. *The RUSI Journal*, *157*(5), 32–45. https://doi.org/10.1080/03071847.2012.733104

Seedat, S., Nyamai, C., Njenga, F., Vythilingum, B., & Stein, D.J. 2004. Trauma exposure and post-traumatic stress symptoms in urban African schools: Survey in Cape Town and Nairobi. *British Journal of Psychiatry*, *184*(2), 169–175. https://doi.org/10.1192/bjp.184.2.169

Seelinger, K.T. 2015. Domestic accountability for sexual violence: The potential of specialized units in Kenya, Liberia, Sierra Leone and Uganda. *International Review of the Red Cross*, *96*(894), 539–564. https://doi.org/10.1017/S1816383115000090

Sheely, R. 2016. Regimes and randomization: Authoritarianism and field research in contemporary Kenya. *Social Science Quarterly*, *97*(4), 936–952.

Shildrick, T., & MacDonald, R. 2013. Poverty talk: How people experiencing poverty deny their poverty and why they blame 'the poor'. *The Sociological Review*, *61*(2), 285–303. https://doi.org/10.1111/1467-954X.12018

Shleifer, A. 2009. Peter Bauer and the failure of foreign aid. *Cato Journal*, *29*(3), 379–390.

Sifuna, D.N. 2006. A review of major obstacles to women's participation in higher education in Kenya. *Research in Post-Compulsory Education*, *11*(1), 85–105. https://doi.org/10.1080/13596740500507995

Silvestri, G., Wittmayer, J., Schipper, K., Kulabako, R., Oduro-Kwarteng, S., Nyenje, P., Komakech, H., & Van Raak, R. 2018. Transition management for improving the sustainability of WASH services in informal settlements in sub-Saharan Africa—an exploration. *Sustainability*, *10*(11), 4052. https://doi.org/10.3390/su10114052

Simister, J.G. 2010. Domestic violence and female genital mutilation in Kenya: Effects of ethnicity and education. *Journal of Family Violence*, *25*(3), 247–257. https://doi.org/10.1007/s10896-009-9288-6

Simon, T., Goldberg, A., Aharonson-Daniel, L., Leykin, D., & Adini, B. 2014. Twitter in the crossfire—The use of social media in the Westgate Mall terror attack in Kenya. *PLoS One*, *9*(8), 1–11. https://doi.org/10.1371/journal.pone.0104136

Singer, H.W. 1989. The African food crisis and the role of food aid. *Food Policy*, *14*(3), 196–206. https://doi.org/10.1016/0306-9192(89)90037-7

Sinha, P., Dissanayake, K., Mahwera, D., & Kahabi, C. 2012. Creating a global vision for sustainable fashion. *Pakistan Textile Journal*, *61*(1), 46–54.

Snowdon, B. 2009. The Solow model, poverty traps, and the foreign aid debate. *History of Political Economy*, *41*(1), 241–262.

Soini, E. 2005. Changing livelihoods on the slopes of Mt. Kilimanjaro, Tanzania: Challenges and opportunities in the Chagga home garden system. *Agroforestry Systems*, *64*(2), 157–167. https://doi.org/10.1007/s10457-004-1023-y

Somerville, K. 2011. Violence, hate speech and inflammatory broadcasting in Kenya: The problems of definition and identification. *Ecquid Novi: African Journalism Studies*, *32*(1), 82–101. https://doi.org/10.1080/02560054.2011.545568

Ssewanyana, D., Mwangala, P. N., Marsh, V., Jao, I., van Baar, A., Newton, C.R., & Abubakar, A. 2018. Young people's and stakeholders' perspectives of adolescent sexual risk behavior in Kilifi County, Kenya: A qualitative study. *Journal of Health Psychology*, *23*(2), 188–205. https://doi.org/10.1177/1359105317736783

Starkey, J. 2013. Twins, 14, reunited with British mother after Kenya kidnapping. *The Times*. https://www.thetimes.co.uk/article/twins-14-reunited-with-british-mother-after-kenya-kidnapping-2xjz70zhhgk

Stephens, E.C., Nicholson, C.F., Brown, D.R., Parsons, D., Barrett, C.B., Lehmann, J., Mbugua, D., Ngoze, S., Pell, A.N., & Riha, S.J. 2012. Modeling the impact of natural resource-based poverty traps on food security in Kenya: The crops, livestock and soils in smallholder economic systems (CLASSES) model. *Food Security*, *4*(3), 423–439. https://doi.org/10.1007/s12571-012-0176-1

Suchman, L., Hart, E., & Montagu, D. 2018. Public–private partnerships in practice: Collaborating to improve health finance policy in Ghana and Kenya. *Health Policy & Planning*, *33*(7), 777–785. https://doi.org/10.1093/heapol/czy053

Sun, J.Y. 2019. 'Now the cry was Communism': The cold war and Kenya's relations with China, 1964–70. *Cold War History*, *20*(1), 39–58. 10.1080/14682745.2019.1602120

Swart, E. 2013. Doing survival strategies for coping with gender-based violence in Kenya's Kibera slum. *Affilia—Journal of Women & Social Work*, *28*(1), 40–50. https://doi.org/10.1177/0886109912470111

Tadjbakhsh, S., & Chenoy, A.M. [1965] 2006. *Human Security: Concepts and Implications*. New York: Routledge.

Taka, M., & Northey, J.A. 2020. Civil society and spaces for natural resource governance in Kenya. *Third World Quarterly*, *41*(10), 1–18. https://doi.org/10.1080/01436597.2020.1783996

Taylor, C.F., Pevehouse, J.C., & Straus, S. 2017. Perils of pluralism: Electoral violence and incumbency in sub-Saharan Africa. *Journal of Peace Research*, *54*(3), 397–411. https://doi.org/10.1177/0022343316687801

Taylor, J., Bradbury-Jones, C., & Lund, P. 2019. Witchcraft-related abuse and murder of children with albinism in sub-Saharan Africa: A conceptual review. *Child Abuse Review*, *28*(1), 13–26. https://doi.org/10.1002/car2549

Terada, Y., Evans, D., & Mwaniki, D. 2017. Planning for the integration of refugee and host communities in Turkana County, Kenya. *Forced Migration Review*, *55*, 52–54.

Tharoor, I. 2015. Kenyans ridicule CNN report calling their country a terror hotbed. *The Washington Post*. https://www.washingtonpost.com/news/worldviews/wp/2015/07/23/kenyans-ridicule-cnn-report-calling-their-country-a-terror-hotbed/

The Advertiser. 2007. Oil man's Kenya robbery ordeal. 1 State Edition. https://search-proquest-comlibraryproxygriffitheduau/docview/355027287?pq-origsite=summon&https://searchproquestcom/central

The Economist. 2002. Nairobbery: Crime in Kenya. *The Economist*, *364*(8285), 50.

Trainor, A.A., & Graue, E. 2014. Evaluating rigor in qualitative methodology and research dissemination. *Remedial & Special Education*, *35*(5), 267–274. https://doi.org/10.1177/0741932514528100

Turner, S. 1998. Global civil society, anarchy and governance: Assessing an emerging paradigm. *Journal of Peace Research*, *35*(1), 25–42. https://doi.org/10.1177/0022343398035001003

Twisselmann, B. 2005. Africa's medical brain drain: Summary of responses to recent editorial on stopping Africa's brain drain. *BMJ*, *331*(7519), 780–781. https://doi.org/10.1136/bmj.331.7519.780-c

Uche, C. 2015. Lonrho in Africa: The unacceptable face of capitalism or the ugly face of neo-colonialism? *Enterprise & Society*, *16*(2), 354–380. https://doi.org/10.1017/eso.2014.31

Ude, P.U., & Njoku, O.C. 2017. Widowhood practices and impacts on women in sub-Saharan Africa: An empowerment perspective. *International Social Work*, *60*(6), 1512–1522. https://doi.org/10.1177/0020872817695384

UN. 2017. *Human Security and Agenda 2030*. Human-Security-and-the-SDGs.pdf (un.org)

UNHCR. 2020a. *DR Congo Emergency*. United Nations High Commissioner for Refugees. https://www.unhcr.org/en-au/dr-congo-emergency.html

UNHCR. 2020b. *Kenya-Figures at a Glance*. United Nations High Commissioner for Refugees. https://www.unhcr.org/ke/figures-at-a-glance#:~:text=In%20addition%2C%2076%20Ethiopian%20refugees,28%2C500%20Ethiopian%20refugees%20in%20Kenya

UNICEF. 2017. *Situation Analysis of Children and Women in Kenya, 2017*. United Nations International Children's Emergency Fund. https://www.unicef.org/kenya/media/136/file/SITAN-report-2017-pdf.pdf

UNICEF. 2018. *Kenya*. United Nations International Children's Emergency Fund. https://data.unicef.org/country/ken/

UNICEF. 2020a. *What We Do*. United Nations International Children's Emergency Fund. https://www.unicef.org/what-we-do

UNICEF. 2020b. *A Profile of Female Genital Mutilation in Kenya*. United Nations International Children's Emergency Fund. Profile-of-FGM-in-Kenya-English_2020.pdf

Unver, O., Kay, M., Chavva, K., Amali, A. A., Pek, E., & Salman, M. 2020. Development for water, food and nutrition in a competitive environment - How NGOs and CSOs are reshaping traditional farmer irrigation advisory services. *Irrigation and Drainage*, *70*, 431–447. https://doi.org/10.1002/ird.2444

van Stapele, N. 2016. 'We are not Kenyans': Extra-judicial killings, manhood and citizenship in Mathare, a Nairobi ghetto. *Conflict, Security & Development*, *16*(4), 301–325. https://doi.org/10.1080/14678802.2016.1200313

Verster, P. 2015. A Christological approach to poverty in Africa: Following Christ amidst the needy. *Hervormde Teologiese Studies*, *71*(1), 1–8. https://doi.org/104102/hts.v71i1.2090

Vimefall, E., Andrén, D., & Levin, J. 2017. Ethnolinguistic background and enrollment in primary education: Evidence from Kenya. *African Development Review*, *29*(1), 81–91. https://doi.org/101111/1467-826812241

Vorhölter, J. 2012. Negotiating social change: Ugandan discourses on Westernisation and neo-colonialism as forms of social critique. *The Journal of Modern African Studies*, *50*(2), 283–307. https://doi.org/10.1017/S0022278X12000055

Waller, R. 2012. Pastoral production in colonial Kenya: lessons from the past? *African Studies Review*, *55*(2), 1–27, https://doi.org/10.1353/arw.2012.0039

Wallis, W. 2003. Kenya terror attacks 'planned from Somalia'. *Financial Times*. https://search-proquest-comlibraryproxygriffitheduau/docview/228798849/fulltext/66AF1C022AF14D3CPQ/1?accountid=14543

Wamagatta, E.N. 2009. British administration and the chiefs' tyranny in early colonial Kenya: A case study of the first generation of chiefs from Kiambu District, 1895–1920. *Journal of Asian & African Studies*, *44*(4), 371–388. https://doi.org/10.1177/0021909609105090

Wamboye, E., Adekola, A., & Sergi, B.S. 2014. Foreign aid, legal origin, economic growth and Africa's least developed countries. *Progress in Development Studies*, *14*(4), 335–357. https://doi.org/10.1177/1464993414521526

Wang, Q., Fu, A.Z., Brenner, S., Kalmus, O., Banda, H.T., & De Allegri, M. 2015. Out-of-pocket expenditure on chronic non-communicable diseases in Sub-Saharan Africa: The case of rural Malawi. *PLoS One*, *10*(1), 1–15.https://doi.org/10.1371/journal.pone.0116897

Wanjiru, J. 2018. Inclusive education for internally displaced children in Kenya: Children perceptions of their learning and development needs in post-conflict schooling. *International Journal of Child Care & Education Policy*, *12*(1), 1–18. https://doi.org/10.1186/s40723-018-0046-1

Were, V., Buff, A.M., Desai, M., Kariuki, S., Samuels, A., ter Kuile, F.O., Phillips-Howard, P.A., Kachur, S.P., & Niessen, L. 2018. Socioeconomic health inequality in malaria indicators in rural western Kenya: Evidence from a household malaria survey on burden and care-seeking behaviour. *Malaria Journal*, *17*(1), article 166, 1–10. https://doi.org/10.1186/s12936-018-2319-0

Weststrate, J., Dijkstra, G., Eshuis, J., Gianoli, A., & Rusca, M. 2018. The sustainable development goal on water and sanitation: Learning from the millennium development goals. *Social Indicators Research, 143*(2), 795–810. https://doi.org/10.1007/s11205-018-1965-5

Wethal, U. 2019. Building Africa's infrastructure: Reinstating history in infrastructure debates. *Forum for Development Studies, 46*(3), 473–499. https://doi.org/10.1080/08039410.2019.1616609

Whittaker, H.A. 2012. The socioeconomic dynamics of the Shifta conflict in Kenya, c. 1963—8. *The Journal of African History, 53*(3), 391–408. https://doi.org/10.1017/S0021853712000448

Whitty, M.T. 2018. 419 – It's just a game: Pathways to cyber-fraud criminality emanating from West Africa. *International Journal of Cyber Criminology, 12*(1), 97–114. https://doi.org/10.5281/zenodo.1467848

Williams, P.D. 2016. AMISOM under review. *The RUSI Journal, 164*(1), 40–49.

Winter, S., Dzombo, M.N., & Barchi, F. 2019. Exploring the complex relationship between women's sanitation practices and household diarrhea in the slums of Nairobi: A cross-sectional study. *BMC Infectious Diseases, 19*(1), article 242, 1–13. https://doi.org/10.1186/s12879-019-3875-9

Wolff, E.A. 2020. The global politics of African industrial policy: The case of the used clothing ban in Kenya, Uganda and Rwanda. *Review of International Political Economy, 28*(4), 1–24. https://doi.org/10.1080/09692290.2020.1751240

Workneh, M.A. 2020. Gender inequality, governance, and poverty in Sub-Saharan Africa. *Poverty & Public Policy, 12*(2), 150–174. https://doi.org/10.1002/pop4.278

World Health Organisation. 2018. *Kenya*. World Health Organization. https://www.who.int/countries/ken/e

Wrong, M. 2014. Everyone is corrupt in Kenya, even grandmothers. *Foreign Policy*. https://foreignpolicy.com/2014/05/06/everyone-is-corrupt-in-kenya-even-grandmothers/

Xinhua News Agency. 2017. Kenyan police foil Al-Shabaab attack in border town. *XinhuaNet*. http://www.xinhuanet.com/english/2017-09/22/c_136630515.htm

Yiwei, W. 2018. Debt trap label hides anxieties of developed nations. *Global Times Business*. https://www.globaltimes.cn/content/1129244.shtml

Zgheib, N. 2020. EBRD and Oxfam to strengthen community resilience. *European Bank*. https://www.ebrd.com/news/2020/ebrd-and-oxfam-to-strengthen-community-resilience.html

Zhang, K.H. 2010. How does globalization affect industrial competitiveness? *Contemporary Economic Policy, 28*(4), 502–510. https://doi.org/10.1111/j.1465-7287.2009.00153.x

Index

African natural resources, 8
aid administration cost, 77–79
aid controversies, 69–74
aid dependency, 74–77

border security, 33
brain drain, 13, 63–65
bureaucracy, 77–79
bypass theory, 5, 81–82

child safety, 12, 13, 24–27
civil society organisations, 82–84
climate change, 13, 21–22
colonialism, 22, 45–65
crimes, 35–38
cultural beliefs and practices, 38–40, 42

destruction of local markets, 61–63
development problems, 8–14
divide and rule, 54–56
donor fatigue, 74–77
draining african resources, 45–48

education, 2, 12, 22–25, 51
epidemics and diseases, 9, 29

food security, 19–22

gender inequality, 11–12, 41–44, 50–54
genocide, 14, 15
governance, corruption, 14, 69–74

health, health systems, and wellbeing, 27–30
human dignity, 7
human rights, 17
human security, 7–14

imperialist practices, 9
impunity, 37, 39
intergovernmental organisations, 14, 74, 95
international community responsibility to protect, 14

land alienation, 45–48

missionary work, Christianity, 50–54

neo-colonialism, 45–65
non-governmental organisations, 2–4, 84–89

political intolerance, 30–32
Politics of international law, 14–17
poverty, 9, 14, 19–30, 45, 67
proliferation of small arms, 10
purchasing power, 21

qualitative research methodology, sample, 3–5

regional and global partnerships, 89–90

sexual- and gender-based violence, 41–44

terrorism, 33–35
the millennium development goals, 16
three Kenyan monsters, 31
torture and trauma, 48–50

violent conflicts, 30–32

witchcraft induced violence, 10–11
world order, 10

About the Author

John Bosco Ngendakurio, PhD, was born in Burundi, a small country in East Africa, in 1980. He lived, studied, and worked in Norway until 2010, when he migrated to Australia. In Norway, he published his first book in 2009 (Ngendakurio, JB 2009, "Kryssild- Mitt liv som flyktning- Burundi- Tanzania- Norge," *Lunde Publishers* (OSLO, Norway) (Translated title: Crossfire- my life as a refugee- Burundi-Tanzania- Norway). This is a semi-biography about the journey of Burundian refugees from Burundi to Norway via the refugee camps in Tanzania. Ngendakurio has completed the following degrees:

- PhD in International Law (2021): Griffith University, Australia. Thesis: The Impact of Foreign Aid on Human Security in Kenya (Directors: Associate Prof. Georgina Murray, Prof. David Peetz)
- Master of Arts (Research) (2017): Griffith University, Australia. Thesis: Congolese Men and Women of Good Hope: The Legacies of refugee camps for work market readiness in Hyper-Diverse Cities (Directors: Associate Prof. Georgina Murray, Associate Prof. Robert Mason)
- Master of International Relations (2015): Griffith University
- Bachelor of International Relations (2014): Griffith University